History
TODAY

Helen Cadbury

Helen Cadbury
Unashamed

A Gospel-shaped heart in
the famous chocolate family

Janice L. Pibworth

DayOne

© Day One Publications 2023
ISBN 978-1-84625-763-6

UK trademark number 1448790.
British Library Cataloguing in Publication Data available
Published by Day One Publications
Ryelands Road, Leominster, HR6 8NZ
Telephone 01568 613 740 FAX 01568 611 473
email—sales@dayone.co.uk
website—www.dayone.co.uk

Cover design by Kathryn Chedgzoy
Printed by 4edge

To my husband, Nigel, who has been my encourager throughout life.

Endorsements

While some will luxuriate with a bar of chocolate, I have found Christian biography feeds my heart, encourages my zeal and causes me to thank my Lord for all that He has done through His people. The Victorian era was rich with men and women who loved their Saviour and did exploits for Him. Years ago I read the biography of Charles Alexander, song leader for the R.A.Torrey meetings. Now we have one of Alexander's wife, Helen Cadbury, who was an extraordinary woman in her own right. In this detailed life story, we capture a picture of someone who experienced the sorrows of so many Victorians, yet prayerfully maintained a sacrificial life of evangelism and philanthropy. Read and be blessed. Chocolate will never be the same again, but nor will be your appreciation of zealous Christianity.

Roger Carswell, evangelist and author.

Helen Cadbury gave heart and soul to everything she did. Whether encouraging her school friends to live the gospel in their daily lives, giving her nieces the run-around in a game of croquet, or gathered by the US Railroad singing 'God be with you till we meet again'. Janice Pibworth has captured the commitment and joyful purpose of her life.

Mary Penny, great niece of Helen Cadbury.

After years of careful research, Janice Pibworth offers a masterful account of a long-neglected Christian. The life of Helen Cadbury Alexander Dixon could have been told as a chocolate heiress who married two influential evangelical revivalists, Charles Alexander and then A. C. Dixon. Happily, the reader is rewarded with much more—a deep and thoughtful exploration of her personal trials, philanthropic work, and lasting influence through the Pocket Testament League.

Kevin Mungons, Moody Publishers, Chicago.

Who does not love Cadbury's chocolates? Yet few among those of us who love the fabulous products of this world-famous chocolatier know anything about the Quakers who founded and maintained this family business. Janice Pibworth's biography of Helen Cadbury opens up the story of one of the children of this Christian family. Her story is a great witness to the glorious God she served for most of her long life. Highly recommended!

Dr Michael Haykin, professor of church history, The Southern Baptist Theological Seminary.

My thanks go to the many institutions which have supplied me with resources for my research but also to the many individuals who supported me throughout my work on Helen Cadbury.

- Ancestry.com—has given me access to various family trees and family connections.
- Archive.org—has been a good source of old and out of print material.
- Evangelical Library—has been a great source of old magazines and newspapers of the time in which to find reports.
- Findagrave.org—the website has been a source of accurate information. Myra Mason has personally visited Helen's and Charles' grave on my behalf and taken photographs.
- Hymnary.org—has been a wonderful site for discovering not only hymns but information about their authors and composers. Dianne Shapiro from this site has been so helpful with quick and well-informed responses to my queries.
- Library of Birmingham, The Cadbury Collection—has a collection of resources about the Cadbury family.
- Moseley History Society—Fiona Adams has sourced information for my research.
- National Library of Australia—has supplied some information from the book, *Fred P. Morris and other Bendigo Hymnwriters* by Keith Cole, (Keith Cole Publications, 1989).
- The Pocket Testament League—their information about Helen as the originator of the Pocket Testament League and their sources of testimonies about the significance of the work has been useful.

- The staff at the Moseley Hall Hospital and the Uffculme Centre were most helpful in showing me around and giving me information.
- Wisconsin Historical Society—Gayle Martinson, the reference librarian kindly copied for me the 'University Baptist Church, historical sketch, 1917–1926' by Helen C. A. Dixon.

The following individuals have been a great help and inspiration for me in the writing of the book:
- Nick Bradley, a great nephew of Helen Cadbury, supplied me with original material, especially Helen's and Charles' personal correspondence. These were a surprise find and have given me a real insight into their personal lives.
- C. Mary Penny, Helen Cadbury's great niece has contributed to my research with her personal reminiscences of Helen Cadbury and her family, as well as supplying original documents, photographs and memorabilia, and her own mother's copy of 'The Nieces' scrapbook'. These have been invaluable.
- Kevin Mungons—the backlist curator for Moody Publishers, and also a writer, has sourced various materials for me, and has kindly endorsed my book.
- Matt Baalham, librarian at Tyndale House, Cambridge was a help in accessing the booklet: *When Home is Heaven*, from the Cambridge University Library.
- Clare Baalham, a freelance editor, was a great help in proofreading and giving editorial advice.

- Roger Carswell has encouraged me to write this biography and has kindly written an endorsement of it.
- Thank you to Dr Michael Haykin for his foreword and recommendation.
- Helen Clark, my editor has been an invaluable help.
- Thank you to Clare and Debbie, my daughters, and their husbands for their interest and support.
- Finally, thank you to my husband Nigel, who has sustained me in this work and has often said, 'I have a book to help!' He has been a great supporter and encourager not only in this work but in our marriage and my spiritual life.

Contents

Contents

Foreword

British Quakers—Cadbury's of Birmingham, Rowntree's of York, and Fry's of Bristol—have had a longstanding connection with cocoa, which they saw as an ethical alternative to alcohol as a beverage. This marvellous biography concerns the first of these Quaker families, the Cadburys, and one of them, in particular, Helen Cadbury (1877–1969), who, by God's grace, had a remarkable life. Her parents, Richard and Emma Cadbury, were ardent Christians and Helen thus knew the blessing of a Christian upbringing in what she later described as 'an ideal Christian home'. Converted in her teens, she was involved in founding what would become known as the Pocket Testament League (PTL and now also known as Bridge Builders). She was married in later life to Charles Alexander, the famous gospel singer, and, after his death in 1920, she married the Fundamentalist leader A.C. Dixon. She was active in both of these men's global ministries and, after their deaths, she wrote important biographies of both of them. When Dixon died in 1925, she continued to be active in various Christian endeavours and the exercise of hospitality to the end of her long life.

I was drawn initially to this marvellous study of Helen Cadbury's life through a personal connection with Cadbury's chocolates. My mother left Ireland around 1950 to work for a number of years at Cadbury's in Bournville. It was there that she met my father at a dance. And subsequent to their marriage, I was born in Birmingham, Helen Cadbury's hometown. A much deeper reason for my interest in Helen Cadbury's story, though, is that it is a clear testimony to the way that God can powerfully use the life of a person committed to living for his Kingdom and for his glory. I am sure my next Cadbury's chocolate bar will not be consumed without thanking God for the Cadburys and for the witness of Helen's life!

Michael A. G. Haykin
Professor of Church History,
The Southern Baptist Theological Seminary,
Louisville, Kentucky
August 29, 2023

Timeline for Helen (née) Cadbury Alexander Dixon

1799 b. Priscilla Ann Dymond (1799–1828).

1801 b. John Cadbury (1801–1889).

1805 b. Candia Barrow (1805–1855).

1826 m. John Cadbury and Priscilla Ann Dymond (1799–1828).

1832 m. John Cadbury and Candia Barrow.

1835 b. Richard Cadbury (1835–1899).

1838 b. Elizabeth Adlington (1838–1868).

1846 b. Emma Jane Wilson (1846–1907).

1854 b. Amzi Clarence Dixon (1855–1925).

1855 d. Candia Barrow (Richard's mother).

1861 m. Richard Cadbury and Elizabeth Adlington

1861 Cadbury business given to Richard and George Cadbury.

1862 b. Barrow (1862–1958).

1864 b. Alice died aged 7 months.

1865 b. Jessie (1865–1956)

1867 b. William (1867–1957).

1867 b. Charles McCallon Alexander (1867–1920).

1868 b. Richard (Junior) (1868–1935).

1868 d. Elizabeth Cadbury, Richard's first wife

1871 m. 25 July Richard Cadbury and Emma Jane Wilson (2nd move to Wheeley's Road).

1872 b. Edith (1872–1951).

1875 Richard Cadbury and family move to Harborne Road.

1877 b. 10 January Helen Cadbury (1877–1969).

1878 b. Margaret known as Daisy (1878–1972).

1879 Bournville factory.

1880 Charles Alexander's conversion—public confession 1881.

1883 Richard Cadbury and family move to Moseley Hall.

1884 b. Beatrice (1884–1976).

1886 d. Mrs Irene Steddom Chapman (1860–1886).

1887 d. George Cadbury's wife

1889 d. John Cadbury

1889 Helen's conversion.

1891 m. Barrow married Geraldine Southall.

1891 Uffculme move.

1893 Official start of the Pocket Testament League by Helen Cadbury.

1897 Richard Cadbury and family's first tour to Holy Land and Egypt.

1898 Bournville's Almshouses built, and Friends' Hall and Institute.

1899 Richard Cadbury and family's second tour to Holy Land and Egypt.

1899 d. Richard Cadbury.

1899 8th April, funeral of Richard Cadbury at Lodge Hill Cemetery.

1901–1903 World Tour—Torrey/Alexander.

1904 Torrey/Alexander Mission to Birmingham.

1904 Engagement of Charles McCallon Alexander and Helen Cadbury.

1904 m. 14th July. Charles and Helen travel to America and Helen becomes American citizen.

1905 'Tennessee', the name of Helen's and Charles' home, is built in Birmingham, England.

1905 m. Helen's sister Daisy to Dr Neville Bradley.

1905 Arrive in Liverpool—marriage celebration for the poor.

1905 Helen ill.

1905 Daisy and her husband, Neville Bradley, go to Pakhoi as missionaries.

1905–6 Charles' missions to UK and America.

1906 Helen's biography of Richard.

1906 Cruise for Helen's recuperation to China to see her sister, then onto Australia. Charles' eye accident at Pakhoi.

1907 April, return home from Australia via Vancouver and New York.

1907 d. of Emma Cadbury, Helen's mother, on board ship returning home from China.

1907 Funeral of Emma Cadbury at Lodge Hill Cemetery, Birmingham.

1907 Uffculme given to Barrow but he declined it. It was used for adult education and handed over to Birmingham City Council in 1916.

1907–9 Chapman/Alexander missions in USA; PTL work and conferences.

1908 Official start of the American Pocket Testament League.

1909 Tours to Australia, China, Korea, Philippines and Japan.

1909 Helen and Betsy have a holiday on the Isle of Wight.

1910 Cardiff mission, early 1910.

1910 Missions in America.

1910 Charles' appendicitis in America.

1910 Helen pregnant.

1910 Chapman remarries.

1911 Baby boy born and died. Inscription on family grave, Lodge Hill Cemetery, 30.6.1911.

1911 Death of Charles' sister-in-law, wife of his brother, Homer; death of Helen's nephew, Arthur, son of Richard.

1911 Chapman/Alexander mission Northern Ireland.

1911 m. Beatrice (Betsy) in December to Cornelis Boeke.

1912 Beatrice and Cornelis (Kees) go as missionaries to Lebanon.

1912–13 Missions in Australia and New Zealand. Helen has appendicitis in Australia.

1913 Return from New Zealand, via Vancouver.

1913–14 Harkness resigns as pianist and Barraclough replaces him.

1914 Scottish missions.

1914 Summer holiday in Cornwall.

1914–18 World War 1.

1914 WW1 camps and PTL work.

1914 Visiting America, late in the year.

1915 Due to return on Lusitania but stayed on in USA; Helen based in Larchmont.

1915 Daisy ill in Canada.

1916 Charles' accident—glass severed an artery. After recovery continued missions.

1917 Barraclough conscripted Voke his replacement.

1918 Armistice. Various missions.

1918 25th Dec 1918, d. Dr Chapman.

1919 Summer back to England. Helen visits Beatrice in Holland. Nieces' house party. PTL work.

1920 Maclean's New Year visit to 'Tennessee'. American missions. British meetings.

1920 October, Charles' suspected heart attack. Virgo's wedding, 12th October—Charles is best man. That night Charles dies. His funeral is at Lodge Hill Cemetery, Birmingham.

1920 Helen writes Charles' biography.

1923 A. C. Dixon (Clarence) meets Helen.

1924 25th January, wedding of Clarence and Helen; return to Baltimore, America. Summer at 'Tennessee'. Visits to Sweden and

France. Return to 'Tennessee', then back to Baltimore.

1925 Clarence ill, died 14 June.

1925–38 Helen travels between America and England.

1927 Researching University Baptist Church, Baltimore, for a booklet Helen was writing about the church and a biography of Clarence. The University Baptist Church in Baltimore still exists today.

1928 d. Reuben Archer Torrey, (1856–1928)—Charles' partner in the Torrey-Alexander missions.

1928 First International Pocket Testament League Meeting at 'Tennessee'.

1936 Helen becomes a British citizen, again.

1939–1945 'Tennesse', Helen's home—a home for refugees.

1961 d. Robert Harkness—his remains are at Charles' grave.

1967 Helen becomes the President of the Stirchley Women's meeting at the age of 90.

1967 Helen's 90th birthday celebration.

1969 Death of Helen, buried at family grave Lodge Hill Cemetery, Birmingham.

Family tree

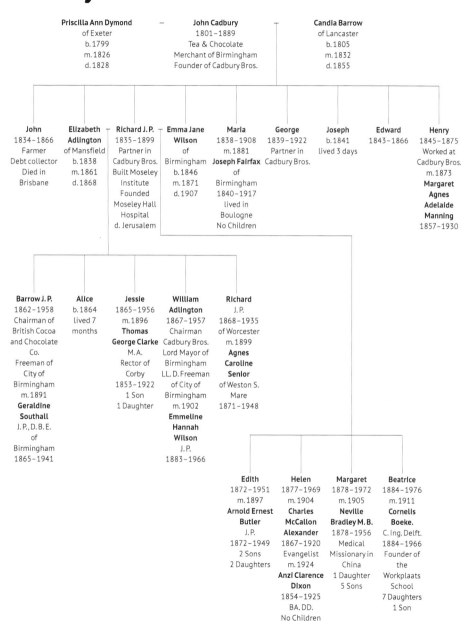

Priscilla Ann Dymond	—	John Cadbury	⊤	Candia Barrow
of Exeter		1801–1889		of Lancaster
b. 1799		Tea & Chocolate		b. 1805
m. 1826		Merchant of Birmingham		m. 1832
d. 1828		Founder of Cadbury Bros.		d. 1855

John
1834–1866
Farmer
Debt collector
Died in
Brisbane

Elizabeth
Adlington
of Mansfield
b. 1838
m. 1861
d. 1868

Richard J. P.
1835–1899
Partner in
Cadbury Bros.
Built Moseley
Institute
Founded
Moseley Hall
Hospital
d. Jerusalem

Emma Jane
Wilson
of
Birmingham
b. 1846
m. 1871
d. 1907

Maria
1838–1908
m. 1881
Joseph Fairfax
of
Birmingham
1840–1917
lived in
Boulogne
No Children

George
1839–1922
Partner in
Cadbury Bros.

Joseph
b. 1841
lived 3 days

Edward
1843–1866

Henry
1845–1875
Worked at
Cadbury Bros.
m. 1873
Margaret
Agnes
Adelaide
Manning
1857–1930

Barrow J. P.
1862–1958
Chairman of
British Cocoa
and Chocolate
Co.
Freeman of
City of
Birmingham
m. 1891
Geraldine
Southall
J. P., D. B. E.
of
Birmingham
1865–1941

Alice
b. 1864
lived 7
months

Jessie
1865–1956
m. 1896
Thomas
George Clarke
M.A.
Rector of
Corby
1853–1922
1 Son
1 Daughter

William
Adlington
1867–1957
Chairman
Cadbury Bros.
Lord Mayor of
Birmingham
LL. D. Freeman
of City of
Birmingham
m. 1902
Emmeline
Hannah
Wilson
J. P,
1883–1966

Richard
J. P.
1868–1935
of Worcester
m. 1899
Agnes
Caroline
Senior
of Weston S.
Mare
1871–1948

Edith
1872–1951
m. 1897
Arnold Ernest
Butler
J. P.
1872–1949
2 Sons
2 Daughters

Helen
1877–1969
m. 1904
Charles
McCallon
Alexander
1867–1920
Evangelist
m. 1924
Anzi Clarence
Dixon
1854–1925
BA. DD.
No Children

Margaret
1878–1972
m. 1905
Neville
Bradley M. B.
1878–1956
Medical
Missionary in
China
1 Daughter
5 Sons

Beatrice
1884–1976
m. 1911
Cornelis
Boeke.
C. Ing. Delft.
1884–1966
Founder of
the
Workplaats
School
7 Daughters
1 Son

Preface

Often in research, you are met with unexpected dead ends but, also, unexpected avenues open up. While I was looking into the life of Ada Ruth Habershon, a Christian hymn writer and Bible scholar, I investigated her hymn-writing partnership with Charles McCallon Alexander. Charles McCallon Alexander was an American singing evangelist who was married to Helen Cadbury. Helen Cadbury was the daughter of Richard Cadbury of the famous Cadbury chocolate business. A new avenue of discovery opened up: this time into the life of Helen Cadbury. Helen had the benefits of a loving Christian, Quaker family, who had the financial means to help others. She mixed with the poor and the affluent alike. Women, at that time, had limited roles in public life, yet, by working behind the scenes, Helen was able to influence many for good, worldwide. She also affected the lives of many in her own 'world'—her home in Birmingham, which was called 'Tennessee'. It was at her home that she entertained many thousands of guests over her long life. Through her two marriages— which were to Americans—she travelled the world in her husbands' preaching capacities and experienced periods of revival in the gospel. Her most significant legacy was the *Pocket Testament League*. The Pocket Testament League grew from an idea she formed during her teenage years: Read, Carry and Share the Word of God. Since its formation, the League has circulated millions of copies of Scriptures throughout the world.

**HELEN CADBURY ALEXANDER
DIXON (1877–1969)**

Introduction

The expression, 'a chocolate soldier', means a person who melts 'under the heat' of trials and difficulties. In this biography, we discover Helen Cadbury Alexander Dixon, the daughter of Richard Cadbury of the famous Cadbury's chocolate manufacturing business, was definitely no chocolate soldier when it came to coping with trials and difficulties. Alongside her husband, she travelled the world and was engaged in evangelistic campaigns. Busy schedules and often relentless pressure, concentrated during these times of world missions, were a necessary part of this work. Her dedication and tireless work on the hymn-book production of the *Alexander's Hymnals*, and the associated issues of copyrighting, was immense. There were endless demands on her time, effort and emotions in her devotion to philanthropic work and especially the work in the slums.

She experienced family bereavements in the deaths of her father and mother and her beloved first husband, Charles McCallon Alexander, the famous singing evangelist, as well as her second husband, Clarence Amzi Dixon, a preacher and evangelist. Helen loved children, yet she was to suffer the devastating loss of her only baby and the continuing childlessness throughout the rest of her life. She underwent various trials of her own illnesses and also cared for others during their illnesses, accidents and deaths.

A constant flow of visitors to her home was her normal way of life but, with it, came the demands of entertaining them and it even included almost adopting some of them. She had an unfailing preoccupation of sharing the gospel and her Saviour to as many people as possible—significantly through her idea of the *Pocket Testament League*. *The Pocket Testament League*'s work continues today in reaching millions with the Scriptures, throughout the world. After widowhood for a second time, she went on to live for a further forty-three years, maintaining some of her work almost until the end of her life, at the age of ninety-two. Helen Cadbury Alexander Dixon wanted to serve her Saviour, the Lord Jesus Christ, and to reach others with the gospel. She was no chocolate soldier in seeking to live out these purposes. Her signature Bible reference was Romans 1:16: '*For I am not ashamed of the gospel of Christ: for it is the power of God unto salvation to everyone that believeth; to the Jew first, and also to the Greek.*'

1 Helen's family background

Helen Cadbury was no chocolate soldier, but she was the daughter of the famous Richard Cadbury (1835–1899), who, in partnership with his brother, George (1839–1932), ran the famous Cadbury's chocolate manufacturing business. Helen was the second daughter of Richard Cadbury and his second wife, Emma, and was born in Birmingham on 10 January 1877. Richard Cadbury already had five children[1] with his first wife, Elizabeth: Barrow; Alice, who had died at the age of seven months; Jessie; William Adlington; and Richard (Jnr). Richard's first wife, Elizabeth (née Adlington, 1838–1868), died ten days after the birth of their youngest child, Richard (Jnr), when she was just thirty years old. Richard was distraught at the loss of his wife and left with four motherless children, the eldest being just six years old.

Helen's grandfather, John Cadbury (1801–1889), and family

To discover more about Helen's life, we need to retrace our steps in time to her grandfather, John Cadbury, and her father, Richard's early life. Richard's parents were John Cadbury (1801–1889) and Candia née Barrow (1805–1855), and he was their second son. John, Helen's grandfather, and his brother, Benjamin, had set up a cocoa and drinking chocolate manufacturing business in Birmingham. Being from a Quaker household, they encouraged, through their café, the drinking of cocoa and chocolate as an alternative to alcohol. Helen's grandfather, John, experienced sadness in his early married life. His first marriage was to Priscilla Ann Dymond (1799–

1828) but they only had two years of married life before her death. After four years of loneliness, he remarried. His new wife, Candia Barrow (1801–1855), was a relative by marriage, who John met while visiting family in Lancaster. She came from a wealthy merchant family that also owned ships and was involved in foreign trade. They married in 1832 and they had seven children[2]: John, Richard, Maria, George, Joseph, Edward and Henry—although one of their sons, Joseph, only survived three days. Richard had one sister, Maria, and had great companions in his brothers, who were often found running around the garden twenty-one times to complete a mile. Richard's father, John, walked before breakfast and returned home by 7am, ready for a Bible reading with the family and his breakfast, and then he was at work by 9am.

Richard's sister, Maria, lived with her father in the family home, in Calthorpe Road, and cared for John, especially after her mother's death. With most of John's children having left home, he moved into a smaller property, which he had built along with another house on his grounds. These two properties were in the back garden of Calthorpe Road and were fronted onto Harborne Road. Later in life, John Cadbury insisted that Maria should be free to marry, even though she was living with her father and caring for him. Maria married Joseph Fairfax and the two of them then lived with her father. Due to being married late in life, Maria was unable to bear children and they remained childless. At the time of Richard's bereavement, George, Richard's brother and business partner, still lived with his father and sister, and Richard's children had a second home at their grandfather's house.[3]

Helen's father, Richard Cadbury (1835–1899)

Helen was described in her childhood as being full of fun, which seems to have been something she inherited from her father. According to Richard's brother, George, Richard was a very good-natured child who was full of fun and a practical joker. As a young boy, Richard was athletic; later he would captain the Edgbaston football and hockey teams and he also enjoyed cricket. He loved the outdoor life, appreciating nature, enjoying the garden and pond at their home, but he was also interested in music. Richard, as a child, loved sailing as well. Although he had an aptitude for most athletic activities, one of his real loves was for ice skating and, as soon as there was ice, he would be seen with his ice skates. He would often rise at 5am so that he could have two hours' skating before work. On one occasion, he rescued a friend who had fallen through the ice by knotting handkerchiefs together and stretching across the ice to pull him to safety.

Richard's conversion

Helen, writing later in her father's biography, spoke of her father's conversion, which he had shared with her when she herself had become a Christian:

> In a home so full of beautiful Christian influences, it was natural that Richard's mind should turn with simple directness to the things of God, for as soon as he was old enough to understand anything he had been told of the love of Jesus. His little heart was very tender, and one day, when he was about five years old, he ran to his own small bedroom, and kneeling down, asked the Lord to forgive him and be his own Saviour.[4]

Again, later Helen wrote that the secret of his fruitful life was his abiding in Jesus Christ,[5] and that his devotion was to God and the Bible. Richard was desirous that all the board[6] schoolchildren in Birmingham and the district should have a Bible. Therefore, he undertook the presentation of a Bible to each child which amounted to tens of thousands; in each Bible he enclosed a slip which said:

> I present you with a copy of the Holy Scriptures, in the hope that you will read a few verses every day. May the grace of the Lord Jesus Christ and the love of God and the communion of the Holy Ghost be with you all!
>
> Your friend,
>
> Richard Cadbury
>
> Jesus said, I am the way, the truth, and the life: no man cometh unto the Father, but by me (John xiv. 6) Search the Scriptures; for they are they which testify of me.[7]

The emphasis and importance of the Scriptures would find its fulfilment in Helen's later work with the *Pocket Testament League*. Her father's example made such an impact on her life and the life of many others.

The Cadbury business

In 1861, while their father John was still alive, the Cadbury business was passed into the hands of the two brothers, Richard and George. Their mother had died in 1855 and his father never really recovered from her death. The business had real difficulties making ends meet. Both Richard and George ploughed their inheritance from their mother of £5,000 each into the success of the business, leaving Richard with only £150 after five years. The brothers then wondered whether they ought to take up other occupations, as the business was an uncertain prospect. George considered a tea business in the Himalayas and Richard, land purveyance. But there were better times for the Cadbury business ahead.

George used his business qualities to develop the purchasing and development side of the business. Richard's business prowess was in sales and later advertising—particularly the use of travelling salesmen called 'travellers'. Some of these salesmen travelled to Australia and other parts of the world to promote their products. In 1864, the tide turned on the business and it started making a profit. Then, in 1866, with the improvements in the manufacture of drinking chocolate and cocoa, a by-product was made of cocoa butter and it was from this that Richard and George developed the now well-known Cadbury's chocolate bars and confectionery. 1866 saw the end of the adulteration of chocolate with its various additives. Later Richard, with his advertising strategy, created the saying, 'Absolutely Pure. Therefore Best', as their motto. As with any business, it had its ups and downs, but overall sales flourished.

> The brothers were at once curiously like and unlike. Richard's was the more restful temperament. He gave his life to good works with quiet, unambitious devotion, but he was not indifferent to aesthetic interests. He had a delicate taste for art, wrote much verse, chiefly of a religious character, delighted in sketching, had something of the collector's passion, and a love for discovering the records of the family.[8]

The idea of using boxes for chocolates was developed by Richard and the decorative lids first appeared in 1868. Richard even used his artistic talents for the illustrations, using his children as models, as well as scenery from Switzerland. Richard enjoyed travelling and he particularly appreciated the beautiful scenery of Switzerland and the opportunity for one of his favourite pastimes: climbing. As a promoter and advertiser, Richard had already used his artistic and entrepreneurial talents in the labels for their products. Considering their plain lives as Quakers, Richard overthrew the ideas of plainness when it came to these chocolate boxes.

> To strike a real note of luxury, Richard decided that some of the Fancy Boxes should be covered with velvet, lined with silk and included a mirror. In every way Cadbury's chocolate was to stand for quality.[9]

Some of these boxes were collected by children so they could keep the decorations or were used by adults for keepsakes. It was Richard who came up with the idea of heart-shaped chocolate boxes, which became popular as a Valentine's gift. The business also developed to produce its own tins, boxes and cards. In 1879, they opened a new factory in a leafy area south of Birmingham to improve the lives of their workers. They believed in the efficiency of the business as well as the welfare of the workers. This became the Bournville site and village with its well-built houses, each with its own garden, as well as public spaces. The factory was often referred to as a 'Factory in a Garden'. It provided facilities such as a canteen, swimming pool and sports ground for the workers. Employees were taught to swim in the firm's swimming pool. An innovative practice was introduced, granting the workers bank holidays and half-day holidays on a Saturday.

Richard's philanthropy

As a Quaker, Richard was a philanthropist and he was referred to by some as the 'Prince of Philanthropists'. His philanthropic work was the fruit of his own faith in Christ. He knew that his good works were not the means of making him right with God but the outcome of it. Christ was the true foundation of his life and he would exhibit this in all aspects of his life, including his business life. Initiating many improvements for the workers at the factory, he introduced adult education for the employees. This was to become one of his chief interests in life. He was also involved with the Temperance Movement as well as other charities.[10] His philanthropic work was a vast catalogue of activities, societies and welfare agencies. His Sundays consisted of an early morning school, the Friends' meeting at 11am and an evening meeting at Highgate (the 'slum' mission hall), and there would often be a children's school in the afternoon. One of his real passions was education for the poor and uneducated and he had been the main driving force in building an Institute for Adult Education, which cost almost £40,000. The Friends' Hall and Institute comprised of a hall which held 2,000 people and had thirty-seven classrooms, a gym and bathrooms, with thousands attending the various classes.[11] While designing a new home for his family, he arranged for Moseley Hall, which had been the family home, to be donated as a convalescent home for children.

Richard's first wife

Richard was married to Elizabeth Adlington (1838–1868) in 1861 at Mansfield. She and her parents were Quakers. Richard had a small house at 17, Wheeley's Road, Edgbaston, where he enjoyed creating a garden for his wife and their future family. As already stated, they had three sons: Barrow, William and Richard, and two daughters,

Jessie and Alice, who had died aged seven months. Elizabeth died at the age of thirty, surviving only ten days after the birth of their youngest son, Richard.

Richard's widowhood

For three years, Richard was a widower and the children remained without a mother. During this time, he enlisted the help and advice of an older widow, Mrs Emma Wilson (1822–1917). Mrs Wilson had been working at the Bishopsgate Street Creche with Richard Cadbury. Richard, who had started the creche, had known personally all the difficulties and demands of bringing up children, running a home and his business with his brother George. Richard realized the tremendous stresses and strains that the women at the factory had in caring for their own children while working. He had seen young toddlers roaming the back streets, uncared for, so he rented a small property with advice from his friend, Mrs Wilson, and a creche was set up. Richard employed staff to run it and Mrs Wilson helped in the appointment of Mrs Dyson as the matron. They started with just five children who were bathed, cared for and provided with toys for the day. It became so popular that Mrs Wilson was able to start a women's meeting to apply Christian principles to home management and to encourage abstinence from alcohol.

Mrs Wilson was a Christian who had had her own difficult trials in life. Married at the age of eighteen, she was then widowed at the age of thirty-nine, in 1861, and left with seven[12] of her own children—four boys and three girls: Ashlin, Hannah, Emma, Samuel, Alice, John, William (or Willie). Being unable to support all the family, the children were split up. The eldest, Ashlin, went to live and work in

Brazil; Hannah went to live with a friend/aunt, Miss Hellena Richardson in Bristol, and became like an adopted daughter; and Samuel went to New Zealand. The three youngest—Alice, John and William (Willie)—stayed with their mother until the boys were old enough to attend the Blue Coat School, a charitable institution, while Emma went to a school in Wolverhampton. Later, she went to Switzerland to learn languages in order to become a governess, where she stayed with 'Aunt' Richardson's friend. John later joined the Friends and became a medical doctor and a missionary in Madagascar.

It was a natural progression for Richard to go from a working partnership and mutual Christian faith with Mrs Wilson to ask her to become his housekeeper. He had employed her at the creche and she was responsible for the mothers' meeting there and he respected her enough to have her as his housekeeper. And so, along with a nurse, a cook and a domestic servant, she helped run the household and look after Richard's young children, although Richard's father and his sister Maria were also involved.

Notes

1 Richard's children from his first marriage were Barrow (1862–1958), Alice (b. 1864, lived 7 months), Jessie (1865–1956), William Adlington (1867–1957) and Richard (1868–1935).

2 John (1834–1866), Richard (1835–1899), Maria ((1838–1908), George (1839–1922), Joseph (b. 1841 lived 3 days), Edward (1843–1866) and Henry (1845–1875).

3 According to the 1871 census, Barrow and Jessie, the two older children, lived with their grandfather and aunt Maria but some secondary sources say that the younger children lived with these relatives. Helen Cadbury, in

her biography, *Richard Cadbury of Birmingham*, writes that all the children lived with their father, but the census shows that, in Richard's household, his two youngest children lived with him, and he employed a housekeeper, a nurse, a cook and a domestic servant—presumably the nurse was for the youngest children.

4 Alexander, Helen Cadbury, *Richard Cadbury of Birmingham*, (London: Hodder and Stoughton, 1906), p. 46.

5 Ibid., p. 426.

6 Board schools were state run schools which made education available for all children.

7 Ibid., p. 335.

8 Gardiner, A. C., *Life of George Cadbury*, (London: Cassell and Company Limited, 1923), p. 23.

9 Cadbury, Deborah, *Chocolate Wars: from Cadbury's to Kraft—200 years of sweet success and rivalry*, (London: Harper Collins, 2010 imprint), p. 75.

10 Examples of his associations: YMCA, Medical Mission, British and Foreign Mission, the Police Mission, The Peace Society.

11 Alexander, Helen Cadbury, *Richard Cadbury of Birmingham*, p. 382.

12 Helen Cadbury, in her father's biography, says Mrs Wilson was a widow left with six children—it could be that the older boy Ashlin was already independent.

2 Helen's mother: Emma Jane Wilson

Mrs Wilson's second daughter, also called Emma but with the middle name of Jane (1846–1907), had been studying in Switzerland for several years. On returning to England in the autumn of 1870, she visited her mother, and she naturally became involved with the Richard Cadbury family. She was extremely fond of children and soon became attached to Richard's children as a mother figure. It was through this close relationship with the children and spending time with the family that she developed an attachment to Richard. Richard found her to have a sweet personality and she had a 'flower-like face, with its appealing blue eyes and frame of waving golden hair',[1] which attracted her to him.

Within weeks of Emma's first visit in the autumn of 1870, Richard and Emma's relationship developed and they became engaged in the October. On 2 November 1870, Richard wrote a note to Emma and the following extract demonstrates his love for her:

> I think I told you that I could not see how it was possible to love you more than I do, but I think now I shall love you more deeply as I know you better, and can more fully sympathise in your joys and your troubles.[2]

Emma's mother, Mrs Wilson, was delighted with the new relationship and could see how their attachment and love had developed. For the sake of propriety, Richard moved out of his home so that Emma could stay in the home with her mother rather than returning back to Switzerland. They were to be married in the following year.

Richard had expressed not only his love for her but his concerns about any anxieties she may have about becoming a mother to his children. He wrote on November 10th, 1870:

I feel how heartily you have entered into the thought of fulfilling the duties of a wife, and I may also say of a mother of the little motherless ones, and I feel assured that God will help you to fulfil your trust. I am so glad of your letters, which breathe so much love to me. They are like so many stepping-stones across a broad river, until I meet you once again in that land of bright and happy days.[3]

Richard and Emma Cadbury around the time of their wedding

Religious differences

Although Emma had been brought up as a Nonconformist, and had attended a congregational church, it was while she was at school that she was influenced by the preaching of Alexander Baring-Gould (1814–1899), an evangelical Anglican in Wolverhampton. She took Confirmation classes and accepted Christ as her own personal Saviour. Later, she decided to join the Church of England.

Richard was a Quaker and yet, although Emma and Richard had different church affiliations, they shared the same common saving faith in Christ, each knowing the reality of having their sins forgiven. Before they were married, Richard expresses in another note, written to Emma on 6 November 1870, the differences of religious practice but how they had the same saving faith in the Lord Jesus Christ:

> I will strive all I can to make you happy. All my enjoyment will be yours, and I do not believe my pledge to love and cherish you for ever can be broken by anything below. I have begun to read the Church Services, and will tell you more when we meet. It is such a comfort to me to have the prospect of joining you in worship next Sunday. It seems such a bond of union for the soul, to worship together the one great Father of all; and although I cannot understand the efficacy of priestly ordinations, yet it makes me very happy to think that we can both own the one great Sacrifice for sin, through whom alone we can find atonement and by whom alone we can approach God's mercy seat (Heb. vii. 26–28).[4]

He then recounts a visit which he had made to a Quaker meeting and says that he would be delighted to introduce her to his Quaker friends.

Richard's own Quaker religious practices were quite different from Emma's original Nonconformist background, let alone her present Anglican services. Although they were both Christians, Richard wanted to explain some of his Quaker beliefs to Emma before they were married and, in this extract, he attempts to present his ideas:

> November 15th. In our conversation together you asked me respecting our disuse of ritual service in the Society of Friends, and I told you that I thought it might be better not to trouble you about such things at present; but I have since thought that perhaps you would be puzzling yourself over it, and wondering how as a Christian,

professing my entire belief in the Scriptures as the Word of God, I could omit them. If it would be any comfort to you I will gladly write them down for you in a simple way. Religion seems to me such a work of God's Holy Spirit in the heart, that although we may reverently thank Him for many ways in which Christ has been revealed to us as the only means by which our guilt can be washed away, yet these can be of no avail unless blessed by the great Giver, and unless we open the door of our hearts to receive Him, who has been knocking there until 'His head is filled with dew and His locks with the drops of the night.' This is the glorious promise: 'If any man hear My voice and open the door, I will come in to him and will sup with him, and he with Me.' With what joy, then, shall we open the gates for the Lord of Glory to enter in. I shall always think of this when I read the beautiful piece we sang together, 'Abide with me'; it is so full of that feeling of peace and rest, which will rejoice our hearts when other comforts fail, knowing that if we will receive Christ He will make His abode with us (John xiv. 23).[5]

In another extract from a letter to his future wife, on 31 January 1871, he wrote:

I read the collect you spoke of in your letter, and thought it a very beautiful one. How often we need to be reminded that this is not our rest, and that while we are here temptations and trials will be our lot. I am so glad that we can tell one another our thoughts without reserve, and feel very jealous to disturb your restful and believing heart; and yet, dearest, I long that the foundation of our faith should be a reality. Not that I doubt for a moment that yours is a sure reality indeed, I long for your pure spirit and humble faith; but I do at the same time look at the help you speak of with some doubt, because I fear we may, to some extent at least, rest on them and feel satisfied that we have done something ourselves towards our salvation, instead of trusting altogether in the Almighty Arm and in the efficacy of the gospel, and the new dispensation in which all rites which typify cleansing and sanctification have received their full accomplishment in the blood shed on Calvary. It is by this alone we can know our sins to be washed away. It is the natural tendency of man to trust in his own deeds and sacrifices for gaining his salvation; but unless they are the result of a humble and contrite heart, they are not acceptable to God.[6]

Later he adds:

Your love and your religious faith have drawn me very near to you, and if it be still God's will that different paths are chosen for us to the one source of everlasting joy, we shall be sure to meet there, and perhaps in God's love and mercy He may still see fit to join us in the same path, for some steps of our earthly pilgrimage, before we meet on that heavenly shore.[7]

These extracts reflect his full assurance of salvation in Christ alone and his confidence in the faith of Emma. Yet, he is not afraid to confront the problems of religious rites and in adding these to salvation by Christ alone and in reality, by these additions, nullifying the self-sufficiency of Christ's atonement. These words also reflect his tolerance of others' choice of different denominations, as long as he was united with the believers of faith in Christ alone. He was not going to force Emma to become a Quaker and he respected her choice and regarded her as free to make that choice without pressure from himself. He did at the same time acknowledge that he would love her to be on the 'same path' as him. On another occasion he says, 'I do so like your way of speaking on the points of doctrine on which we may differ,'[8] which reflects his graciousness and his respect for Emma. They each attended the other's meetings: the Quaker morning meeting and the Anglican evening service but, within two years of their married life, Emma chose to become a 'Friend' and eventually they were united in being Quakers.

Richard and Emma's wedding

Within a year of their first meeting, Richard and Emma were married on 25 July 1871 at Tyndale Chapel, Redland, Bristol, near the home of 'Aunt' Richardson. Miss Hellena Richardson (1819–1890),[9] who was a spinster, had 'adopted' Hannah Wilson, Emma's elder sister, when their father had died, and their mother was left with seven children and little money. It was this 'Aunt' Richardson who had arranged for Emma, at the age of twenty, to stay in Switzerland with a family friend, Frau Meyer. Frau Meyer treated and loved Emma as a younger sister, providing her with free board and lodging and undertaking to pay her tuition fees; at one time, when Emma was ill, she even nursed her. Richard's and Emma's wedding took place in Bristol, as 'Aunt' Richardson had insisted that Emma 'married' from her home in Westbury upon Trym. Emma stayed before the wedding with her 'Aunt',[10] where both her sister, Hannah, and her brother, John (John Henry), lived.[11] Emma and Richard were married at Tyndale Chapel according to the rites of the Baptists.[12] Emma's two older brothers were unable to attend, as was Richard's father, but the two youngest brothers, John and William attended; Emma's two sisters, Hannah and Alice, and Richard's sister, Maria, were bridesmaids and Emma's younger brother, John Henry, was a witness to the marriage. John Cadbury, Richard's father, was able to meet up with them at Birmingham railway station as they made their way to the Lake District for their honeymoon. He gave them grapes from his own hothouse and a purse of gold coins to Emma as a wedding gift. After their honeymoon, they returned to their new family home in Wheeley's Road with the four children to start their life together. Much later, Richard's daughter, Edith, would move back into this house with her husband Arnold Ernest Butler as her own marital home.

Emma's character and home life

Emma's elder sister wrote the following description about her:

> She was always a child of the home; helping with her younger brothers and sisters; quiet, orderly, methodical. We were a family of seven, some of us rather tempestuous spirits and the chief thing about my dear sister that stands out in memory is her gentle speech and manners and her sweet looks, which won people's hearts and gained her many friends. [13]

Helen inherited some of her mother's (Emma's) characteristics and not others! Helen was certainly orderly and methodical, but one would not call her quiet!

Aged just twenty-five, Emma became not only the wife of the famous Cadbury businessman but a loving and caring stepmother to his four children. Later, Richard and Emma went on to have four daughters of their own: Edith, Helen, Margaret (known as Daisy), and Beatrice (known as Betty or Betsy). Emma, as well as becoming a stepmother and a mother, was hospitable in using her home for the benefit of those in 'less favourable conditions'. Their home was opened up for Sunday schools; various classes and meetings from a range of denominations; the Band of Hope; Christian workers; and endless visitors. (The Band of Hope was a group advocating temperance or the abstinence from alcohol, with the aim of particularly helping working class children who suffered from detrimental effects on their lives.) The family saw another addition to them, this time of Emma's young nephew, the son of her youngest brother William, who had become a Quaker and was now a missionary in Madagascar. This again showed how their home was used for the benefit of others. Later in Emma's life, after the demands of bringing up the children grew less intense, Emma developed her own role outside the home. This is a catalogue of the work with which she was involved: mothers' meetings; adult school and Institute work and its associated Christian work; the mission hall; president of the convalescent hospital; president of the temperance society; trustee of the almshouses; mission work to the police; and an elder of the Friends Society, to name some of them! Helen certainly followed in the busyness of her mother's example. Having seen Christian home life lived out in practice, she followed in her parents' footsteps, providing hospitality to so many in her own home. Helen and her future husband's motto of, 'Each for the other and both for God', was certainly the cornerstone of her parents' marriage.

New family home

Before their marriage, Richard wanted to provide a fresh start for their married life and a new home for the family, which meant leaving his present home with the incumbent sadness associated with it. He sought to purchase a new property and asked the advice of his father and Mrs Wilson, Emma's mother, who were both happy for him to purchase the property. Richard asked Mrs Wilson, Emma's mother, if the position and outlook of the prospective new home would be to Emma's liking and Mrs Wilson thought that Emma would appreciate it. The new home was only a short distance away from his previous home, which was number 17. They now moved to 26 Wheeley's Road, although it was not number 26 originally as, at the time, it was referred to as Wheeley's Hill and later it was amalgamated into Wheeley's Road. In another letter, Richard comments on his thoughts about the new home and the new life ahead of them, but the extract also conveys something of his love for his children and the interest that Emma had in them, and also some of their characteristics:

> I have again been over the house in Wheeley's Road, with your dear mother, who likes it very much, and thinks you would too. How happy it makes me to think of everything nice for you. The children are very well. Barrow is getting on nicely with his lessons; Jessie is lively and affectionate; Willie, 'the little brother,' is beginning to show real progress with his reading; and Bonny[14] is as sweet as ever.[15]

So, on 22 March 1871, Richard moved into the new home, which would be ready for his new bride after their marriage on 25 July 1871.

The home life of Helen's parents

> Richard Cadbury's home-life preached silent but enduring sermons to many who entered it. Simplicity, but genuine hospitality, unselfishness, and forbearance, earnest ambitions for the good of the world and the glory of God, marked that happy Christian household.[16]

This reference to the Christian characteristics of the home life of the Cadburys is even more poignant in that it was written by Helen, as an adult, when reflecting on her father's life after his death. These are the words of an insider of the household who recognized these Christian qualities and who, in later life, would seek to reflect these in her own home life. Yet, Richard himself acknowledged he had a weakness with his temper and, in her autobiography, Helen mentioned this to reflect not only one of his human weaknesses but also to show his seeking to control it by God's grace:

> Although the hot temper which was naturally part of his energetic nature was usually kept under, flashes of it would occasionally break through. No one was more alive than himself to this weakness, which the grace of God so marvellously controlled in him, and whenever an outburst of impatience did show itself, the humility and gentleness which followed broke everybody down.[17]

Richard and Emma Cadbury, circa 1880

Richard's pattern of life was that he rose early in the morning and exercised. This was followed by breakfast and a family Bible reading before going to work, arriving before 8.30 am so that he could deal with business letters before the 9 am Bible reading with employees. Much later, when Emma and Richard had some of their own children, a snapshot of the happy family life was reflected in a letter which Richard wrote to his wife, who was away collecting Jessie from school:

> Edith was at home to welcome me, and very pleasant it was to see her bright little face. Upstairs I heard the little ones singing, and there they were with nurse round a bright fire, Daisy ready to go to bed, a sweet little angelic picture in her nightdress, and full of love and Nellie [i.e., Helen] singing on the floor, with her shoes and stockings off, as pretty a picture as you could possibly imagine.[18]

Although the family were well off, they sought to live relatively simply and were generous in their giving to others in need, as well as using their home for the benefit others. Helen, having seen these things first hand, certainly implemented the unselfishness of hospitality. Home life seemed to be very happy. People spoke of Richard having a cheerful disposition with some humour; some aspects of these characteristics were inherited by Helen.

Notes

1 Alexander, Helen Cadbury, *Richard Cadbury of Birmingham*, pp. 141–142.

2 Ibid., p. 143.

3 Ibid., p. 144.

4 Ibid., p. 144.

5 Ibid., p. 144–5.

6 Ibid., p. 147.

7 Ibid., p. 148.

8 Ibid., p. 154.

9 Miss Richardson was not a relative but a friend but insisted on being referred to as 'Aunt' Richardson.

10 Hellena Richardson was a great advocate of the temperance movement and the Band of Hope, and had written a children's book based on the evils of drink, which was published by Thomas Nelson.

11 Termed as boarders on the census of 1871 of Hellena Richardson, Westbury upon Trym, Clifton, Bristol, Gloucestershire.

12 Some have wrongly attributed the place of the wedding, either as 'Aunt' Richardson's home or have assumed that, as Emma was an Anglican, it was at a Church of England church, but on the marriage certificate it quite clearly states the place was Tyndale Chapel and the rites of the Baptists. Also, on the certificate it gives Emma's address as the home of Miss Richardson.

13 The Annual Monitor for 1908 GB and Ireland (U.S., UK and Ireland Quaker published memorials 1818–1919 (Ancestry.com)), p. 25.

14 Bonny was the name used for Richard (Jnr), the youngest child from Richard Cadbury's first marriage.

15 Alexander, Helen Cadbury, *Richard Cadbury of Birmingham*, p. 146.

16 Ibid., p. 157.

17 Ibid., p. 200.

18 Ibid., p. 163.

3 Helen and her siblings arrive

By the end of the following year, 1872, a new baby daughter, Edith, was born into the happy home. This was Richard and Emma's first child together.

Richard and Emma's children grew up and when Barrow was eleven, he spent some time in Germany learning the language and continuing his education. Richard valued the knowledge of other languages and the benefits of appreciating the associated cultures. He sought to encourage his children's all-round development by them experiencing life in another country and environment. In 1875, Richard and the family moved to the adjoining property of his father's house in Harborne Road and, later that year, they endured another family sadness when Richard's youngest brother, Henry, who had only been married two years and who had a three-month-old daughter, died of typhoid fever. Henry had joined the company with Richard and his brother, George, only four years previously but, during this time, he had already made his mark there and was loved by the workforce. George and Richard were devastated to lose yet another brother.

In January 1877, there was good news with the safe arrival of Helen. Another daughter for Richard and Emma, Helen was Richard's fourth daughter[1] and Emma's second daughter and child. Eighteen months later, another daughter was born, named Margaret but known as Daisy. The other children were growing up: Barrow, having returned from Germany, went to study in Manchester; Jessie went to the Edgbaston High School for Girls and, later, to the Quaker boarding school, the Mount School, York; William and Richard (junior) went to school in Hitchin. Finally, another daughter would be born to them, called Beatrice (Betty or Betsy). Jessie, being the

Helen Cadbury as a child

eldest daughter, was the first in the family to attend the Edgbaston High School for Girls. This was unusual in that the school had started because Nonconformists, including Quakers, felt that the school curriculum had become sectarian with teaching creeds and catechisms with which they could not agree. Edgbaston High School for Girls had been created as a limited company to opt out of this new curriculum development, to avoid the students having to be taught these sectarian catechisms. Jessie became the first of the daughters to attend this school, with Helen following in her footsteps and later becoming head girl at the school.[2]

Bournville

The children were growing up and Richard and Emma led busy lives. Richard was occupied with work and the new development of the Bournville factory and its associated housing, as well as his adult education work, which included Scripture teaching. There was also his church work; his slum mission work; writing poetry and writing a history of chocolate;[3] research on his ancestry;[4] and his 'Blue Ribbon' (i.e., temperance) work, which developed into the Gospel Temperance Mission. Emma was always supportive of him and his work, especially his Christian work, which would often take him away from the home in the evenings. George was probably the bigger driving force in the development of the Bournville village, although Richard fully supported it, both in its ideas and its finances. (George also survived Richard for a longer time to make an impression on its development.) Richard was the initiator of the development of the almshouses for older, poorer people—mostly retired employees but not exclusively. The thirty-three single-storey houses were centred around a quadrangle lawn and flowerbeds, with an orchard behind the houses where the almshouse occupants could gather the fruit crops for their own use. Each almshouse had a living room, with a curtained-off bedroom and a small kitchen, as well as their own back garden. Although Richard was recognized for his business and philanthropic work, he 'never forgot or neglected his chief object, which was to bring men and women definitely to Christ, finding in His salvation and the guidance of the Holy Spirit the only secret of moral integrity and true Christian living'.[5]

A new home

In 1883, Richard decided that the family would move to Moseley Hall, which was equidistant between the new Bournville factory and the adult education school where he taught. He also wanted the family to move into the countryside. Richard described to them the large lawns, the trees and the fields and the large pool or pond, with the rabbits scampering across the lawns and fields. In fact, the children called the house 'the Bunny House'. Helen was seven years old when the family moved into Moseley Hall. Moseley Hall was a wonderful family home but also a place of service to others. The country house, in its large grounds, was built in 1795 with three storeys and a large portico with four pairs of columns. With its 'spacious rooms, and long, stone-paved passages [it] was full of mystery and delight to the young folk ... It was a house full of surprises. In one room was a cupboard, with mirror panels ... delightful nooks for hide-and-seek'.[6] Richard did not originally purchase the house but rented it. Then, in 1889, he purchased it and, two years later, he donated it to the city of Birmingham for a children's convalescent hospital, once he had finished building a new home for the family. This vast house and land became a wonderful home for the children and was used for entertaining many visitors. Moseley Hall and their next house were to be great examples of how Richard and Emma used their home for Christian hospitality. This would be reflected in Helen's own home, except with one significant, sad difference, described later in this book. A few months after the move, Beatrice, their last child, was born to complete their family.

Home life

The children were made aware of the privileges they had and the service they could provide for those less fortunate than themselves. The children were useful 'workers' in entertaining the many visitors to the grounds of Moseley Hall:

> ... carrying round heavy cans of tea as soon as they were big enough or distributing bags of buns and cakes. They played games with the children from ragged schools, Sunday schools, or bands of hope, and were delighted to look after the babies at a mothers'-meeting party. The little girls and their governess instituted what was known as the

'Poor Class'. They had a list of poor homes in Balsall Heath, including several widows, a few old couples, and a big family or two, which they took under their special care. As there was no school on Saturday mornings, the Friday afternoon was always given up to visiting the 'Poor Class'. Savings were carefully hoarded for the Christmas fund, towards which all the family subscribed. Every opportunity was taken to earn money by picking up apples in the orchard, weeding in the garden, dusting their own rooms and making their beds, so as to swell the funds. Chocolates and sweets were saved, and one of the little girls had a toy chest of drawers full of these trophies in her bedroom, which would often be counted over and longingly gazed at, but were kept uneaten by Spartan efforts. Perhaps they grew stale by the time they were given away, but there must have been a secret flavour about them, absorbed from the childish love that had stored them up. At Christmas times the schoolroom at Moseley Hall would be a scene of suet-chopping, raisin-stoning, currant-washing, and other preparations for the making of Christmas puddings, which, with groceries and other things, were personally delivered at the homes of the 'Poor Class'. The farm cart was lent, piled high with holly and evergreen, with which the children and their governess decorated the often dingy rooms. Once or twice a local chapel was borrowed for a tea-party, with a Christmas tree, and a little meeting to end up with, at which Richard Cadbury and his wife gave their willing help to their children's efforts.[7]

Richard and his wife, Emma, became more concerned about the health of these young, poor children and a desire in their hearts formed for a convalescent home to care for the health of the children and give them an experience of the outdoors. They searched for a suitable property but then realized that, with the lease on Moseley

Hall needing to be renewed soon, Mosley Hall itself fulfilled the requirements for a convalescent home. They started out on the purchase of the property and the twenty acres of land, but not only this; they funded alterations including hot-water heating.

The large pond, which had been built in the extensive grounds of Moseley Hall, was used for boating and swimming and, in the winter, for ice skating. Richard's love for ice skating seemed to have been passed on to his children. What a joy of laughter and fun when the ice was thick enough for ice skating and, on occasions, for a small charge, friends were invited to join them with the monies going to the Gospel Temperance Mission. Helen and her sisters particularly enjoyed being able to show a group of visitors to the summer parties, around the pond. Flowers from the grounds were collected and often distributed to the poor and, when the 'ragged children'—these were destitute children who were supported by charitable institutions—attended the summer parties, they loved the fragrance of the blossoms and the flowers. Richard's eldest son, Barrow, who had joined the Cadbury's chocolate business, celebrated his marriage at Moseley Hall. In fact, his marriage to Geraldine Southall, was the last significant event at Moseley Hall before the family moved to Uffculme.

Happiness and sadness

Family life was pleasant and their home was shared with many others but, during this time, there was family sadness. In 1887, George Cadbury's wife died and left him with five young children. This must have brought back memories of Richard's own experience. Jessie, Richard's eldest daughter, returning from abroad went to

Helen, Emma and Daisy

help with the care of the little ones. In 1889, John Cadbury, Richard and George's father, died leaving a large hole in their lives; Maria, was distraught at the loss of her father, having spent so much of her life caring for him. Soon after her father's death, she and her husband moved away to live in France. John Cadbury, although he had handed over the business to his sons a long time previously, had always been part of it. As head of the business and the family, he was greatly missed and mourned. Richard had learnt so much from his father about family life and carried on the tradition of gathering the family together for weekly meetings.

With all the busyness of life, work, family, education and Christian work, Richard still found time to develop his passion for Palestine, Egyptology, exploration and archaeology, so he joined the Egypt and Palestine Exploration Society. He loved sharing this passion and interest with his family; in fact, for his fiftieth birthday, a celebratory cake in the form of a step pyramid was made with fifty candles decorating it. It was a family tradition for everyone's birthdays to be celebrated with a birthday cake and the relevant number of candles.

Uffculme

When Helen was fourteen years old, a new family home with extensive grounds was built in 1891. The name, Uffculme, was chosen from the Devon village where the Cadbury family had originated. Richard himself had researched his family's ancestry and had meticulously handwritten the Cadbury genealogy in The Family (Cadbury) book. While the project for Moseley Hall's conversion to the children's convalescent home was going ahead, Richard and Emma had looked for suitable new accommodation as a family home. It would have been better if they moved further out into the countryside, with better, healthy living conditions for the family and also nearer to Richard's work. Yet, with all the commitments of his mission work and his regular Highgate adult schoolwork, to which he walked several times a week, it was felt that they needed to stay close by and a plot was purchased not too far away from the Highgate work.

The large family home was built, which accommodated most of the close family members and some more

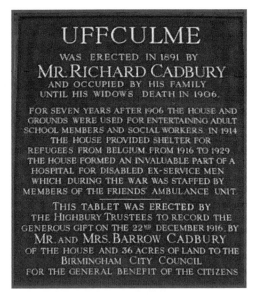

Plaque in Uffculme

Present-day Uffculme, previously Richard Cadbury's family home

distant relatives, including Emma's youngest nephew, Alec, who became part of the family when Emma's brother and wife returned to Madagascar to continue their missionary work. It still allowed them to provide hospitality for their extensive number of visitors. Richard personally designed the layout of the house with the special feature of a great hall. A pipe organ was incorporated into a large window recess. In spite of it being a family home, it appeared in many ways more like an old-fashioned museum with the great hall displaying cases of animals, butterflies and birds alongside statues and various exhibits and curios; yet it still somehow retained a cosy family atmosphere. The children's favourite curio was the grizzly bear which was laid on a sofa, and the children would clamber over it. The hall led into a palm house where the children could talk to a live cockatoo. Uffculme became their new family home, full of laughter, joy and fun. Again, like Moseley Hall, the grounds of Uffculme were used to give poor families an experience of the country air, as well as being used for many Christian groups of various denominations. Instead of tents for the summer garden parties for the poor, tea-sheds were built to provide more substantial facilities—especially useful in the case of bad weather. Helen, later in her adult life, used the same tea-sheds for Christian work.

Holidays

With the busyness of work and life, holidays were a pleasure to be anticipated and then enjoyed. North Wales was one of their favourite places. Llandudno was the site for an early children's work on the beach, which the Cadbury family joined in.

> Nearly every day we have had two services on the sands for children. Mr. Josiah Spiers has come from London especially for the purpose. He was the first promoter of these children's services, and it is a pretty sight to see the children flocking round him from digging on the sand to hear something about the love of Jesus. Some of them (almost all children of well-to-do parents), have never been spoken to about the need of forgiveness and salvation, and I am so thankful to say that many have confessed Christ; some who came to laugh can now thank God that they have found Jesus to be their Saviour.[8]

The family enjoyed climbing the mountains of Wales and also enjoyed the nature surrounding these beautiful places. Cornwall, Scotland and the Yorkshire Moors were favourite venues for holidays. Richard Cadbury and his brother, George, had jointly purchased a property in the Malverns as a holiday home to be used for their families and also to be used by visitors. The property was called Wynd's Point (Wind's Point) and had been the home of Jenny Lind, a famous singer. Lind performed for the famous P. T. Barnum, of Barnum Circus, singing at over ninety-three gala concerts at his musical theatre. The family frequently visited Wynd's Point and it would be a significant venue for various members of the family.

Later in Helen's life, it was used for a significant event—her honeymoon! Some of these family holiday haunts became favourite places for Helen, too, in her later life when she revisited them. Richard had toured Europe earlier in his life and he had visited his sister, Maria, in France. He loved Switzerland, where he could enjoy his favourite pastime of climbing, and he had brought his love of the Swiss scenery to the paintings for the Cadbury chocolate boxes. It is, therefore, not surprising that the family visited Switzerland—on one occasion the party included his wife and his five daughters. Visits to Italy were also made, although Helen did not accompany them, being away at college.

Helen

Helen had been born into a busy family life with a dedicated and hard-working father and a mother who cared for the eight children

Back L-R: Barrow, Richard, Edith, William, Daisy, Richard
Front: Helen, Jessie, Beatrice, Emma

and various visitors. In spite of the busyness of life, Richard always found time for the family but he also knew inner peace with God. In his dressing room was hung part of the hymn, 'Peace, perfect peace, by thronging duties pressed, To do the will of Jesus, this is rest!' Helen grew up having a fascinating, happy and varied childhood with her family, and she mixed with a whole variety of people. She had inherited beautiful 'trusses' of hair like her mother. She was a determined young girl who was bright and had a strong personality, as well as a sense of humour and fun. These qualities would stand her in good stead for her future and she was definitely no chocolate soldier in her temperament. Her musicality was evident: she was an accomplished pianist and violinist as well as having a good singing voice. The family was often heard singing and were even heard singing in the countryside when on holiday. Her parents and family life made indelible marks upon her character and laid foundations and principles which would be evident in her later life; she loved them dearly and admired their examples.

Notes

1 Richard's daughters: Alice, his first daughter, died aged 7 months; Jessie his second daughter—both of these to Elizabeth nee Adlington Cadbury—followed by Edith and Helen to Emma nee Wilson Cadbury and then Margaret (known as Daisy) and finally, Beatrice both to Emma nee Wilson Cadbury. His sons from his first wife: Barrow, William and Richard (known as Bonny when young, then later as Richie or even Dickie).

2 Helen's youngest sister, Beatrice, also attended Edgbaston High School for Girls but Edith, who was not physically strong, was advised by the doctors to live near the sea and, therefore, attended a school at Weston-Super-Mare.

3 Richard's book on chocolate: Cadbury, Richard ('Historicus', pseudo), *Cocoa: all about it*, (Birmingham: Samson, Low and Marston, 1892).

4 His work on pedigree in Cadbury: William A. and Henry J., *The Cadbury Pedigree*, (Birmingham, 1904). (This includes Richard Cadbury's genealogical charts which he researched and are handwritten by him; they form part of 'The Family Book'.)

5 Alexander, Helen Cadbury, *Richard Cadbury of Birmingham*, p.189,190.

6 Ibid., p. 214–215.

7 Ibid., p. 222–223.

8 Ibid., p. 320.

4 A changed life

Helen's conversion

While still young, Helen attended mission halls with her father, where she mixed with many from the slums of Birmingham. On one visit to the mission hall, she was impressed by the changed lives of the people who, from the depths of depravity and destitution, had trusted Christ as their Saviour. It was at one of these meetings, when she was about twelve years old, that she herself realized she needed a Saviour to forgive her sins and to change her life. After the preacher finished sharing the gospel, he challenged the hearers to publicly declare their trust in Christ for their sins forgiven. Helen knew it would be hard to make this declaration in front of her father and others, but she stood up and went into a small room where someone would pray with her. Her father was there, as he normally was, in seeking to help sinners turn to the Saviour and he rejoiced in seeing Helen coming to realize her own need of a Saviour and there, in that small room, he prayed with his daughter.

Later, Helen wrote these words about her conversion:

> If ever a girl was blessed with a Christian father and mother and an ideal Christian home, I was that girl. From my earliest childhood I had not only been taught about the Lord Jesus Christ but had seen Him glorified in the lives around me. And yet I learned from my own experience that the very best home training is not sufficient without a personal acceptance of Christ. People often say that children cannot understand spiritual things, and I remember a friend of mine once

saying to me that she intended never to allow her little girl three years old to even hear the word 'sin'. But I know that these things were very real to me as a child. When I was twelve years old, I remember that for months my heart was heavy and burdened with the sense of unforgiven sin. I longed to be a Christian like my father and mother; but I knew that my will was not fully yielded to God.

My father was a busy man. Although at the head of a great business, his chief aim in life both in his business and outside it was to work for the Lord Jesus Christ in bringing others to know Him. Besides the Mission work in connection with the factory and surrounding village, he had built up a most successful work in a slum district of the city. He had built a Mission Hall in which meetings were held all the year round. Once a year, usually in the autumn, a special effort was made by means of a two-weeks' mission to gather in outsiders, men and women who belonged to no place of worship. Our workers would go into the public houses, night after night, and into the streets, and bring them into the

Helen, Jessie, Edith, Daisy and Beatrice in front

Mission Hall. At such times we children were allowed occasionally to go with our father to the evening meeting. How well my memory takes me back to one night in November, when he took me with him. The Mission Hall was crowded, many of the poor men and women from the streets having come in. I sat at the back of the hall with some of our friends, while my father went on to the platform with the missioner. I remember nothing of the sermon, except that through it all I heard the voice of God speaking straight to my heart. But I do remember one of the hymns that we sang. It was an old-fashioned hymn, perhaps not one that might seem likely to interest a child.

'Free from the law, O happy condition,

Jesus has bled and there is remission;

Cursed by the law, and bruised by the fall,

Christ hath redeemed us once for all.'

I looked about at the faces of the people as we sang. Many were there amongst our workers, whose lives in the past had been as bruised and wretched as some of those whom they had brought from the public-houses that night. But Christ had redeemed them, and as I saw the light on their faces while they sang 'Free from the law', I knew it was more than mere words to them. They were free, and they knew it. A hunger came into my own heart. If only I could sing it as they were singing it. If only I could know, too, that for a certainty I was free from the law. At the close of the meeting an invitation was given for any who would accept Christ that night to signify it openly by rising to their feet. I seemed to forget the people round me. I only knew that God was calling me; and with others in the hall, I rose to my feet. A little later, and those who had risen were invited to come forward to a little room at the back of the platform, where they could have quiet personal conversation and prayer with one of the workers.

Now came a struggle, for I felt all would know me if I walked through the hall, but I half rose to my feet, when one of my friends touched my arm and suggested what was already in my own mind, 'Why not wait till you get home, when you can have a quiet talk with your father and mother!' Then I knew that I must act. For if it was good for these men and women to make an open confession of their need of Christ, then it was good for me, too, for my need was as great as theirs. So, I was given courage to walk through the hall to the little room, which was filled with inquirers and workers. I saw my father in one corner of the room kneeling in prayer with a young man, who had evidently come in under the influence of drink, but was completely broken down. I sat and waited, and in a few moments my father rose from his knees ,and looked across the room. Never shall I forget the light in his eyes as he saw his own little girl sitting there.

He came to me at once, and knelt and prayed with me. For years that dear voice has been silent on earth, but its tender tones are still fresh in my memory as he prayed that God would take and keep my life. From that day a new impulse for living began for me. The joy and peace which God had given me was too good to be kept to myself, and I longed for others with whom to share it.[1]

The beginning of the Pocket Testament League

Having become a Christian, Helen began to avidly read her Bible and she was eager to share her new faith with other girls at her school. As with her father's example of being a 'soul winner', she had the same desire and she prayed about finding opportunities to share the gospel. Her father encouraged her to always share the gospel message based on the Scriptures rather than opinions and arguments. A Christian friend, Florence, and Helen regularly prayed together and sought to witness, which they preferred to do with individuals. They tried to present the Scriptures and felt they wanted to read the Scriptures with people to show that the message was based on the Bible. Florence and Helen kept their Bibles in their desks for this purpose, but they were large and cumbersome; thus, they had an idea of carrying a small, pocket-sized New Testament. Even they were difficult to carry, so they sewed pockets into their clothes to be able to carry around the New Testaments. This was the start of the work which would develop into the *Pocket Testament League* (PTL and now also known as Bridge Builders). Helen, at first, did not find it easy, yet she knew the importance of soul winning. A small group developed and, to be a member of the group, each one had to pledge to always carry at least part of the Bible and read a portion of it every day. For those who joined the Pocket Testament League and who were believers, there was an assumption and encouragement to use the Bible to seek to witness and become 'soul winners'. Helen's father pledged to give a New Testament to any of her fellow students

Helen circa 1896

who enlisted as a member of the Pocket Testament League. By the end of Helen's schooling, there were sixty members. But the work petered out as Helen went on to further education.

Education and theological difficulties

Helen was educated at Edgbaston High School for Girls in Birmingham, where she was head girl and then, went on to further study at The Mount School, York—a Quaker school. At eighteen, Helen studied at Westfield College[2] in London and for the first time in her life she lived independently of her family and their beliefs and the influence of the Quakers. It was here that she met other viewpoints and, especially, different theological beliefs. These centred around questioning the inerrancy of Scripture and adopting the 'liberal theology' and *Higher Criticism* of the time. Here is an excerpt from her biography of her father to explain her thoughts:

> [I] had happened to come into contact with a refined sort of scepticism and a subtle attitude of criticism towards Christian truth, which, added to an intense agony of soul caused by the Armenian massacres, had shaken her hitherto unquestioning faith to its foundations. This was followed by a state of spiritual paralysis, and a cessation of any effort to win souls for Christ.[3]

These ideas were in opposition to her parents' faith. As part of Helen's education, she wanted to go to Germany to study music and, there, she became immersed in the arts. Again, there was a conflict of opinion of the arts and her father wrote to her of his concerns that the Word of God should be the rule of conduct for one's life. Here is an extract of one of her father's letters to her, while she was in Germany, concerning the arts and Helen's lifestyle:

> You are of an age to judge yourself on such matters, and neither mother or I wish to dictate or lay down our will against your well-considered judgement. Nor do I know sufficient of the surroundings and character of such entertainments to go into any details. I have been happy without anything of the kind, and so far our children have not only had happy lives, but lives which have been untainted with the fascination that often draws young girls into worldly life and associations. I want you to feel that we both have every confidence in you, and are quite sure that you will not enter into anything that you know you cannot ask God's blessing upon. This is our safeguard, if we are honest to our convictions and make God's Word our rule of conduct ... Make it a matter of earnest prayer, and God will guide you aright, and then rest assured that we shall not judge you. May the Lord

bless you, my darling, with his richest blessing, and make you still a blessing to others.

With dearest love from us all, your affectionate father.[4]

Helen held onto morality but abandoned many of her previously held beliefs.

Notes

1 Davis, George, T. B., *The Pocket Testament League Around the World*, (Philadelphia: The Pocket Testament League, 1910), pp. 2–5.

2 Westfield College was a small female college in London which had opened in 1882. It was the first of a kind in England to educate women for the University of London degrees. It specialized in the arts and humanities, encouraging academic study beyond the often-domestic training that women of the time received. Later it merged with Queen Mary College and became part of the University of London, as well as becoming co-educational.

3 Alexander, Helen Cadbury, *Richard Cadbury of Birmingham*, p. 289.

4 Fox, Simon, Helen Cadbury and Charles M. Alexander, *A love that embraced the world*, (London: Marshall Morgan and Scott Publications, 1989), pp. 18–19.

5 The death of Helen's father

Travels

Holidays had been an integral part of the Cadbury family life but, with the family growing up and some of the older members now married and with their own children, the family party grew smaller on these family visits. Richard, Helen's father had a keen interest in Egypt and the wonders of the 'Ancient World'. His interest in Egyptology overflowed into the family and became their interest too. Alongside this interest, they had an interest in the Holy Land and the Biblical landscapes. Hence, in 1897, with this keen interest, a desire was fulfilled in a visit to the Holy Land and Egypt, being made by Richard, his wife, Emma, and the four youngest daughters: Edith, Helen, Daisy (Margaret) and Beatrice. Not only was this an exciting adventure, but the journey would also include a tour across parts of France and Italy and along the Adriatic coast. This holiday made such an impact on the daughters with such a contrast not only of the scenery and its beauty but the culture and way of life in such a different setting.

> Words cannot describe the effect on the minds of the six travellers, as day by day new wonders were unfolded before them. The river itself, on whose bosom glided numbers of picturesque boats with crossed, wing-like sails, presented a continually changing panorama, as did the banks on either side. Date palms, tamarind trees, yellow mimosa-bushes, and sometimes a purple drapery of Bougainvillea; camels and buffalos; the creaking wheel of a sakieh, or a shadoof worked by a lithe, brown-skinned Arab to irrigate the cultivated land; women in

coarse blue dresses washing clothes at the river-side, or men filling their water-skins; crowds of native pedlars, beggars, or troops of children calling for 'backsheesh', these were some of the daily pictures on which their eyes rested.[1]

Following the expedition to Egypt, the family travelled to the Holy Land where they were all struck with awe at the sights and the familiar Biblical places such as Jerusalem, The Mount of Olives. Bethlehem, Jericho, Nazareth, the Dead Sea and Jericho. They camped in tents and travelled on horses with mules for their baggage. They visited one of the Friends' Mission near Ramallah and, on the Sunday, Richard Cadbury preached a message through an interpreter. The family enjoyed following the narratives in the Bible referencing them to the places visited. Sketch books and cameras were used to capture their experiences and the flora and fauna was appreciated by all. Another visit to a

Richard, Helen, Margaret and Beatrice on a trip to the Holy Land

Friends' Mission—this time at Brummana in Lebanon—was made, where a Cadbury relative was working in a girls' home. Once again Richard Cadbury spoke at the meetings through an interpreter. The dire needs of the schools and hospital made an impression on the family.

The Friends' Institute and Almshouses

The following summer was spent in Cornwall for a family holiday.

Richard wanted to see the completion of two very important concerns and interests which he had: firstly, the completion of the Almshouses at Bournville; and secondly the completion of the Friends' Hall and Institute, Moseley Road. The latter was an establishment to provide space for the adult schoolwork and the Sunday meetings. In 1898, the work had increased to over 460 men attending the morning school and a large Bible class on Sunday afternoons of about 260, with women numbering 180 and 130 for their separate meetings; over a thousand children attended the Sunday afternoon schools and over 200 people attended the evening meeting. The building was to be used by various other Christian meetings and groups: Christian Endeavour, Band of Hope, Temperance Society, Mothers' Meeting and Bible classes on various evenings. The large hall would hold 2,000 people and there were various other smaller rooms, a gym, bath and changing rooms. The walls were decorated with Scripture texts, which Richard Cadbury had chosen. This was all completed before the end of 1898 and the family were especially pleased as the following year was to be another family expedition to Egypt. The year of 1898 climaxed with a family Christmas.

A family Christmas

Christmas in the Cadbury family had always been a highlight of the year and this year was no exception. Christmas day started early with the children singing carols outside their parents' room, which climaxed in the usual singing of 'Merry Christmas to all'. Richard Cadbury would, then, throw coppers to the children which would be shared among them, with the youngest getting the most! Before breakfast, the family gathered together for their morning prayers followed by a Christmas hymn and a Bible reading of the birth of Christ. Then breakfast followed with Emma, Helen's mother, being given pride of place as it was also her birthday on this day. Her birthday cake was placed in the middle of the table, and her presents were on a chair beside her. Helen's elder sister, Edith, along with her husband and their infant son Dickie, who lived nearby, visited the family to spend Dickie's first Christmas with his grandparents. At ten o'clock the children made their way to the schoolroom where presents were shared with the servants. It was a joyful and happy time together before the other members of the family gathered together in the home. By half past twelve, more guests had arrived to fill Uffculme: Uncle George with his second wife and their, now, nine children; and Benjamin Head Cadbury, a cousin of Helen's father, with his three children. Three of Helen's half-brothers and sister were unable to be there: one was abroad, and one family had an outbreak of whooping cough. So, it was only thirty-four that year that sat down at one o'clock for Christmas dinner!

After dinner, Father Christmas knocked at the front door and was admitted; Richard Cadbury loved appearing in this role and he, then, escorted the children to the study where a Christmas tree was decorated with presents beneath it. Father Christmas and the children danced in a circle before they said goodbye to him. Little did they know that this yearly appearance of Richard Cadbury would never be repeated again. Richard Cadbury, without his costume, then secretly appeared among them, and the children never noticed. Later, the children trooped upstairs to enjoy their presents while the adults had some respite. At six o clock, the whole family and visitors were gathered together again, this time for high tea, followed by games and then, finally, to end the day they all gathered round the organ to sing some hymns before the guests left. Before the children went to bed, everyone had to clear up any mess, as they had been reminded that many had worked hard to make the day such a wonderful celebration and everyone could help to tidy up. Christmas day was an important family day of celebration but life for Helen's father had already been busy with Christmas celebrations elsewhere with various groups that he supported and the work's Christmas party, where 2,000 employees were entertained.

The opening of the Friends' Institute

On December 27th, 1898, about 1,600 people gathered for the opening of the Friends' Hall and Institute—although a formal opening ceremony was planned for May the following year. It had been one of Richard's ambitions to have proper facilities for the adult school and the Sunday work. A surprise presentation was made to him from all those who appreciated and benefitted from this work. Emma, Helen's mother, gave a short speech in which she thanked her husband for their life together and his work for the adult school and the building of this Institute; she said that its purpose was for the praise of God. Richard, then, wished them all a Happy New Year. Again, no one knew at this time that it would be his last formal occasion and that the new year would bring an end to his life.

The Egyptian expedition

The beginning of 1899 was full of preparations by the family for their visit to Egypt and the Holy Land. Helen's father was busy working until the end and was always making sure that things were in order. He had formed a trust for the Institute and the Almshouses and, along with his brother George, papers had been drawn up that, if either of them died, the company would become a limited company. It was as if there was a premonition that things had to be sorted and left prepared for any eventuality. On Sunday 29th January 1899, Richard Cadbury spoke to the whole of the school on the solemnity of the presence of God. For the next couple of days, Richard crammed in various meetings: the Police Institute; the law courts where he was a J.P.; and the Gospel Temperance Mission. Yet he found time to fit in a family dinner party before the family set out on their holiday expedition, on February 2nd. This time there were seven family members in the party: Richard; Emma; Edith and her husband, having left their son with Edith's mother-in-law; Helen; Daisy; and Beatrice.

The first stop was to visit Aunt Maria, Richard's sister, and her husband in Boulogne-Sur-Mer in France. Each family member of the expedition took turns in writing a journal letter for the family members back home. A long journey followed to Egypt and they eventually arrived in Cairo. Having visited two years previously, it seemed familiar but at the same time new. All of them enjoyed the visits to the Sphinx, the Pyramids and the surrounding areas and all tried camel riding! Journeys were made down the Nile and visits to various archaeological excavations. On a return boat journey one Sunday, Richard read his paper on '*The Jewish Race in Egypt*' and, later that evening, the family joined other passengers with hymn singing. Emma Cadbury, Helen's mother wrote in a journal:

> We are all in the best of health and enjoying everything thoroughly. I

wish you could all see father; he is most enthusiastic, taking rubbings and drawings wherever he can. Everyone comes to him for information, and he is looked on as 'the Egyptologist' on the boats. He joins in everything that is going on, and chats with all. He is called all sorts of names by the natives, such as 'Mr Cook', 'Father', 'Baron', and so on.[2]

At this point in time, the whole family was enjoying the Egyptian expeditions. They arrived in Assiut, where they visited the American Mission and its hospital. The hospital was in dire need of financial aid to build more premises and to have better sanitation. Kindly, Richard Cadbury donated to the mission's hospital fund. The day following the mission hospital visit, Richard developed a sore throat and, soon afterwards, Helen came down with similar symptoms and both became very unwell. Both were diagnosed with 'Nile fever', a common complaint, and after a couple of days, with Richard still wanting to press on to the Holy Land, the doctor advised that they would be able to travel and the different environment would be better suited for them both to convalesce. So, the family set out on the steamer journey from Egypt to the Holy Land.

The Holy Land

The journey to the Holy Land was difficult with the steamer carrying a load of cement and its dust aggravated the throat condition. On arrival in Palestine, a two days' car journey from Jaffa to Jerusalem made their health worse and Richard found even drinking milk was difficult with the bad throat condition. Then Beatrice, the youngest of Helen's sisters, became ill. Richard did not want the healthy ones to be restricted to the hotel and, although he was unable to speak, he wrote down all the various places they should visit while he, Helen and Beatrice rested and recovered in the hotel. By Tuesday 21st March, all three were beginning to feel much better. Added to this, there had been some cause for anxiety as they had word back home that the baby of Edith, Helen's eldest sister in this party, had been very ill with her mother-in-law but that day a telegram had been received to say that the danger was over. So, the Tuesday night everyone went to bed feeling much better that these days of anxiety were over. Plans were now altered to include a quieter and slower-paced tour to Bethlehem.

The death of Helen's father, Richard Cadbury

With Helen's parents' usual practice of Bible reading and prayer, which included that night thanksgiving for the recovery of their

Richard Cadbury (1835–1889)

grandson, Richard went to sleep. Emma stayed awake by his side and then, suddenly, Richard opened his eyes but, before she could call for the children, Richard closed his eyes and died. On Wednesday, the church bells rang out the tune for the hymn, 'Thy way not mine'. Sympathy came from various local quarters and the staff at the hospital for the Jews sent messages of sympathy and support. What had been diagnosed as 'Nile throat' was in fact diphtheria. A telegram was sent home to tell the sad news of Richard Cadbury's death, which would come as a shock since the recent letters and messages had been filled with glad news of their expeditions and findings. It was decided by the family that people back in England would want to commemorate his life; therefore, they arranged for his embalmed body to be returned home. Helen was very conscious of the grief of her mother in the loss of Richard but, at the same time, was impressed at how she conducted herself during this period. It was a difficult and arduous journey, but the family met with much sympathy and support on the way. Helen's two eldest half-brothers met the grieving family at Marseilles and accompanied them the rest of the journey back home to Birmingham, where, on April 7th, they arrived safely back at Uffculme. Hundreds of messages of sympathy had poured into the family home from the rich and the poor alike.

Richard's funeral

The funeral took place at Lodge Hill Cemetery in an area set aside for Quaker burials, on Saturday April 8th, 1899; about ten thousand people attended to commemorate his life.[3] A simple Quaker ceremony took place with its initial silence, followed by the hymn, 'Peace, perfect peace', Scripture reading from 1 Corinthians, prayer and silence before Richard Cadbury's brother said:

> 'Thanks be to God, who giveth us the victory through Jesus Christ our Lord'. His voice trembled but grew stronger as he continued. 'Some of us have been helped by the life and faith of our departed brother, some of us have been helped by his words, some of us by his prayers, when he seemed to come into such close union with his God and Father. We are suffering from his loss, but we can rejoice for him … The secret of his fruitful life was his abiding in Jesus Christ … May we who are left for a little longer walk in still closer union with each other.'[4]

Another hymn was sung, and the benediction was given by the Bishop of Coventry.

The impact on Helen of her father's death

Helen was twenty-one when she accompanied her father, Richard, a keen Egyptologist, and some of her family members on the visit to Egypt and Palestine. Although she had been ill at the same time as her father, and her sister Beatrice a few days later, she had recovered. She was, however, stricken by the grief of losing her father in such a sudden and unforeseen circumstance, and in such a faraway place. She had to face a long journey back home with her father's embalmed body and her grieving mother, elder sister Edith and her husband, and her youngest sister, Beatrice, and then, meeting her two eldest half-brothers at Marseilles for the journey home. Life was changing with the loss of her father and there would be more change to come and decisions to be made.

Memorials

Sometime after the funeral, decisions would need to be made—some more urgent than others and some easier than others. One easy decision was to build a new wing, called the Richard Cadbury Wing, for the English Hospital in Jerusalem and a 'Richard Cadbury nursing post' was created for Jewish patients, in honour and memory of her father and to reflect the care and treatment which he received in his last days. Others wanted to have some memorial of Helen's father and donations flowed in to have two busts of him erected: one at Bournville in the girls dining room and the second to be erected in the newly built Friends' Institute Moseley Road—one of Richard Cadbury's main interest. Normally at the end of the year

Richard would hold a Christmas party for the Bournville workers but, for the year of his death, 1899, it was decided that each worker would be presented with a small book entitled, *A Threefold Chord*,[5] containing selected texts for each day of the year. Inscribed inside the cover was written, 'In loving memory of the late Richard Cadbury, with best wishes for the year 1900.'

Other groups who had benefitted from the work and interest of Helen's father requested that they installed memorials for him. The Police Institute funded a memorial tablet; the residents of the almshouses had a picture of him hung in their meeting room with this appropriate text below: 'Inasmuch as ye have done it unto one of the least of these my brethren, ye have done it unto Me.'[6]

It was much later, in 1906, that Helen wrote her father's biography, but I have decided to add the extensive quote from the foreword of the biography to give insights into not only her father but the significant effect his homelife had upon her and the family:

> The Foreword written by Helen Alexander in her biography of her father Richard Cadbury.
>
> Since my father's sudden passing away in Jerusalem, in the spring of 1899, a wish has often been expressed for some record of his life. A period of ill-health, necessitating several months at home, while my husband was continuing his mission work with Dr R A Torrey in America and Canada, seemed like a call to attempt the fulfilment of that wish. Remembering how my father shrank from anything in the nature of eulogy, I have told the story as simply as possible, knowing that facts will give the best insight into his character and desiring that what is told may be stimulating and suggestive in a practical way. It is sometimes the case that those who shine in the eyes of the world are

seen to least advantage in the candid light of home; but much as my father was loved outside, it was in his home that the genuineness of his Christianity was most fully revealed, and the private side of his life is therefore invaded with an object. From generations back he had learned to care deeply for family unity and affection, and there is no doubt that his life and work were greatly influenced by the strenuous example of his father and grandfather. For this reason, it seemed well to give a brief sketch of their lives and activities, and thus introduce some flavour of the vigorous Quaker atmosphere into which my father was born. The keynote of his life was love; he was a genius in the art of loving. His love for God gave balance and sanity to his love for his fellow-men and was the root of the true humility which was probably his other most striking characteristic.

His religious work, philanthropy, or business occupations were never separated into cut-and-dried sections. Through every part of his life, he sought opportunities of bringing souls to God through Jesus Christ. This did not hinder but rather helped him pay wise and thorough attention to what is sometimes termed the secular side of things, and he threw himself with enthusiastic ardour into everything which he undertook. There is not a day when the thought of him fails to uplift and encourage me in all that is best, and the desire to share this helpfulness with others had made the preparation of this book not only a labour of love but of delight. (Birmingham, 1906)[7]

Tributes

The outward show of grief at Richard's funeral was:

A tribute not merely to the splendid philanthropies associated with the name of Cadbury, but also to the singular beauty and sweetness of Richard Cadbury's character. He carried the sunshine with him wherever he went, and combined a simple and unaffected piety with a constant good humour and practical helpfulness that made him universally beloved. His life had been a record of incessant service, and his benefactions were not less generous and widespread than those of his brother, though they followed an earlier model, and aimed less at stimulating social reform and shaping opinion on such subjects as the land and old age pensions, than at alleviating the misery he saw around him. No good cause in Birmingham appealed to him in vain, and among his many considerable gifts to the public, were the conversion of his old home, Moseley Hall, into a convalescent home for children; the erection and foundation of the beautiful almshouses at Bournville; and the building of the Moseley Road Institute for the Adult School movement. His interests were various, but they were all permeated by the one dominating passion of his life, the desire to win men to the faith which shone with such steady radiance in himself.

The maxim 'Live openly' was adopted very deliberately, and the family life was entirely free from those habits of secrecy or exclusiveness so common in the English family. This inherited trait of the brothers had been strengthened by forty years of the closest comradeship in business and in public work. Each was the complement of the other; George intense, original and daring, Richard the steadying and balancing element. Together they formed a remarkable combination, and behind the external differences there was a permanent and fundamental unity of aim.[8]

Helen, in writing her father's biography, summed up its purpose:

If through these pages he, being dead, may yet speak of the Saviour whom he loved and served, this book will have succeeded in the sole object for which he would have been willing that it should be written.[9]

Life at home

In 1899, Helen, now just twenty-two, was faced with choices about her future. She wanted to care for her mother; therefore, she resolved to relinquish her independence and to live with her mother at Uffculme, the family home. Her decision was not only of obligation but of her love for her mother. She was no chocolate soldier in having to face a choice at this important stage of her life, especially coinciding with her own grief at the loss of her beloved father. When she wrote her father's biography, Helen put the following inscription in the front of the book, which shows the affection and respect she had for her mother and the married life of her parents:

> To my Mother, whose radiant married life and whose courage in her loneliness are my constant inspiration.

With the death of Helen's father, and now away from some of the influences of liberal theology, she re-evaluated some of her beliefs and she began reading the Bible again for herself and began to trust it. She immersed herself in the slum mission work with her mother and did not shy away from the hardships of this work:

> [Helen] devoted herself more than ever to religious and philanthropic work with her mother, among the poor of Birmingham. She regularly taught a Sunday School class of 20 young women, training them to become teachers; while on Sunday evenings she conducted a Gospel service for young children at the Friends' Institute. At another Institute erected by her father, she superintended a Working Girl's Club, which had a membership of about sixty, which met weekly.[10]

Helen's mother, Emma, with the loss of her husband and most of the family either married or away from home, threw herself into various interests outside the home. As mentioned earlier, she became busy in her philanthropic work and her slum mission work and became a prolific letter writer. Later, she would continue her interest in travel and visited various parts of the world, but home was always the centre of hospitality and Helen certainly followed in her mother's footsteps in this respect. Helen too, unknown to her at this time, would become a well-travelled person to many parts of the world. Emma would rise early in the morning and spend at least an hour of quiet time reading and prayer; even into old age she continued this practice, even when her family suggested she rested longer in bed! Helen, in her later life even when suffering from arthritis, seemed to have her mother's resilience to keep going. Over the next couple of years, life at the family home changed. Helen's older siblings were now married and had moved out of the family home and her two younger sisters were living away from home. Helen was feeling the loneliness of her personal life with just her mother at home. She wondered whether there would be a future partner for her to share her life and she committed her desires to God in prayer.

Notes

1 Alexander, Helen Cadbury, *Richard Cadbury of Birmingham*, p. 325.

2 Ibid., p. 409.

3 See Appendix 2 of groups which attended Richard Cadbury's funeral on pp. 245–246.

4 Alexander, Helen Cadbury, *Richard Cadbury of Birmingham*, p. 426.

5 *The Threefold Chord*—a precept, a promise and a prayer. From the Holy Scriptures, for every day in the year.

Chapter 5

6 Matthew 25:40

7 Alexander, Helen Cadbury, *Richard Cadbury of Birmingham*, Foreword.

8 Gardiner, A. C., *Life of George Cadbury*, (London: Cassell and Company Limited, 1923), pp. 91–92.

9 Alexander, Helen Cadbury, *Richard Cadbury of Birmingham*, p. 434.

10 Davis, George T. B., *Twice around the World with Alexander, Prince of Gospel Singers*, (New York: Christian Herald, 1907), p. 92.

6 Charles McCallon Alexander: His life before Helen

Charles McCallon Alexander (1867–1920): His family

Charles Alexander, often known as just plain 'Charlie', was born in Tennessee, USA, in 1867 to believing parents. The family were poor farmers trying to recover the land after the turmoil of the Civil War. Charles' father, John Darius Alexander, possessed 'a voice of great sweetness'.[1] Charles said:

> One of the earliest memories I have is of singing Gospel hymns, as we sat around the family fireside in our log home amid the hills of Tennessee. My mother sang sweetly, and my father famous throughout all the region around about as a musical leader. He purchased the first book of Gospel songs that came out when Moody and Sankey were doing their great work ... As soon as I was able to read anything, my father taught me to read music.[2]

Charles' father was an elder at the Presbyterian church and his mother was also a devout Christian who, every evening, would read Christian literature with the family and her favourites were the sermons of D. L. Moody, which became Charles' favourites. Little did Charles know that he would follow in the steps of Moody and Sankey with their evangelistic missions.

Charles' conversion

Charles had personally come to know the Saviour but had not publicly confessed it. In 1881, during a meeting where his Uncle William challenged him about his state before God, his Uncle

William said, 'Charlie ... you love the Lord Jesus Christ don't you?'[3] Charles had been afraid to publicly confess his Saviour in front of others but at the end of the meeting he 'rose and walked timidly to the front at the side of his big uncle and made his first public confession of Christ. With tears of joy, his mother came and kissed him ... The next Sunday he was received into the church by Dr Bartlett ... the pastor of the church at Cloyd's Creek.'[4]

Charles Alexander

In 1884, he was able to see Moody and Sankey for himself when they preached at the Staub's Opera House in Knoxville. At the time of the death of his father, Charles re-evaluated his values in life and decided that he should seek to save souls and to undertake training as part of this. Having decided on training, he attended the Moody Bible Institute, and it was from here that he first sang with A. C. Dixon. Each part of Chicago had been allocated to an evangelist during the World Fair, along with a gospel singer to preach and sing the gospel. The Dean of the Moody Bible Institute at that time was R. A. Torrey, with whom, later, Charles would join in an evangelistic partnership for many years.

Charles frequently worked with people in the slums and benefitted from his experiences of well-known singing evangelists and song leaders. In 1894, Charles joined in partnership with M. B. Williams, an evangelist, for a two-week campaign; due to their success they were invited to many parts of the USA and the partnership lasted six years!

Charles' text: 2 Timothy 2:15

One year Charles, along with a friend, decided they would have a text for that year which was 2 Timothy 2:15 (AKJV): 'Study to shew thyself approved unto God, a workman that needeth not to be ashamed, rightly dividing the word of truth.' They quoted the reference, '2 Timothy 2:15', to each other whenever they met or parted. On one occasion, when Charles shouted it to his friend who was departing on a train a nearby, a hearer having heard it went home and read the Scripture text and from this he sought God and was later converted. Throughout this year, whenever Charles wrote a letter he would write, 'Second-Timothy-Two-Fifteen', and, from then on, his signature always had this reference accompanying it. He was a man focused on the Scriptures and the gospel.

Charles Alexander and Torrey

Torrey, who had been the Dean at the Moody Bible Institute where Charles had attended, had been asked to take some evangelistic missions in Australia. M. B. Williams, who normally worked with Charles, was away and Charles was free, so it was an easy decision for Torrey to ask Charles to accompany him as his song leader.

Torrey

Reuben Archer Torrey (1856–1928) was born in New Jersey. He was a brilliant academic having trained at Yale University, where he was converted. He then went onto Yale Divinity School and, later, to study theology in Leipzig and Erlangen Universities. He married Clara Smith and they had five children. In 1889, he became Dean at Moody's Bible Institute and was involved with Moody's campaign in Chicago. In 1894, he became the minister at the 'Moody Church'.[5]

He was an enthusiastic preacher and personal worker and he preached all over the English-speaking world. In 1912, he became the Dean of the newly founded Bible Institute of Los Angeles, and he was one of the three editors of *The Fundamentals*,[6] along with A. C. Dixon—who was later to become Helen Cadbury Alexander's second husband. He wrote over forty books. The Montrose Bible Conference, North Carolina, was founded by Torrey and it is here that he and his first wife are buried. A memorial stone was erected with the Scripture of 2 Timothy 4:7 engraved on it: 'I have finished my course. I have kept the faith'.

Torrey and Alexander campaigns

When Torrey was invited to go to Australia for campaigns, it was an obvious choice for him to ask Charles Alexander, who had been his student at The Moody Bible Institute. When Charles left the Bible Institute, Torrey continued to trace his success. The way was opened up when Charles' partnership with Mr Williams had a break because Mr Williams was taking a holiday. Thus started the partnership which would last many years. When Charles and Helen married, R. A. Torrey and Mrs Clara Torrey became very close friends, and each husband valued the contribution that they made, not only to them as husbands but to the work that each wife did in the campaigns and personal work. The families enjoyed some holidays together and, at the time of the British campaigns, the Torreys were entertained at Uffculme, Helen's family home, before 'Tennessee'—their own home—had been built, as well as the Cadbury family's retreat at Malvern.

This partnership developed into not only a life-long friendship but as an evangelistic partnership it meant they travelled the world together for many years. It was while in Australia that many other vital friendships were formed: J. J. Virgo (1865–1956)[7] and Robert Harkness (1880–1961)[8] being but two of them. A close friend, George T. B. Davis, who would become a staunch advocate of the Pocket Testament League, described Charles as firstly a believer in prayer and that he had a passion for personal work and the saving of souls. He also had the personal qualities of sympathy, courtesy and kindness along with his buoyancy and cheerfulness which was always exhibited in his radiant smile with an accompanying sense of humour.[9] Praise indeed.

In early 1904, Helen's mother read about the forthcoming Torrey-Alexander Mission to be held in Birmingham, England. Torrey and Alexander, in the last two years, had toured North America, Australia, New Zealand and India and now they had come to the UK to take missions in London, Edinburgh, Aberdeen, Dundee, Belfast, Manchester, Liverpool and Birmingham. Alexander was the singing evangelist of the American Torrey-Alexander evangelistic partnership. He had a good singing voice and was an excellent choir leader with a winsome personality and a desire for soul-winning. He popularized the song called the 'Glory song' through singing it at the various missions; the song had been composed by Charles H Gabriel.

'The Glory Song' by Charles H G abriel[10]

When all my labours and trials are o'er,
And I am safe on that beautiful shore,

Just to be near the dear Lord I adore
Will through the ages be glory for me.

O that will be glory for me,
(O that will be glory for me,)
Glory for me, (Glory for me,)
glory for me! (glory for me!)
When by His grace I shall look on His face.
That will be glory, be glory for me.

When, by the gift of His infinite grace
I am accorded in heaven a place,
Just to be there and to look on His face
Will through the ages be glory for me.

Friends will be there I have loved long ago;
Joy like a river around me will flow;
Yet just a smile from my Saviour, I know,
Will through the ages be glory for me.

Charles Alexander travelled to many parts of the world proclaiming the gospel in word and song.

Helen and Charles' first meeting

On Sunday 17th January 1904, the Torrey-Alexander Mission started in Bingley Hall, Birmingham and ran for four weeks. On the next evening a public welcome was made for the evangelists by the Lord Mayor and various dignitaries including George Cadbury, Helen's uncle. For four weeks the mission continued at Bingley Hall with various other meetings at different times and venues. The mission was successful with thousands attending and many professing conversion. Helen's mother was a supporter of the mission and Helen, with her renewed faith, became a counsellor at the Birmingham meetings at Bingley Hall. In the early days of the mission, Helen's mother had invited Charles to spend one of his rest days at her home. At first, he did not know who she was but, when someone told him she was Mrs Cadbury, he was surprised as he had already been entertained by some of the Cadbury family. The mission was a big success with huge crowds attending and many 'decisions for Christ' being made. It was at the mission that Charles had noticed a young lady, who he later found out to be Helen.

At the last meeting, there was a mob-like situation with crowds not wanting to leave and who were swarming towards the front platform, which could have been dangerous, but Charles with his quick thinking signed to Harkness to play the piano. Then Charles said,

> 'Friends, we must not close such a mission as we have had together like this. I appreciate your love, but I want our last vision to be of Jesus,' then everyone sang:
> 'See from His head, His hands, His feet,
> Sorrow and love flow mingled down.'[11]

The singing continued until the crowds quietly dispersed.

> This scene was being closely observed, from a far distant corner of the great Hall, by a young woman, who had been pleading and praying till the last moment with some factory girls whom she sought to lead to Christ. It was perhaps one of the things that impressed her mostly deeply with the pure aims, and earnest sincerity of the young song-leader, who with a party of his friends had been visiting her mother's home a few days earlier. She had sought to hide, even from herself, the

deep heart-stirrings which had been awakened by the man whose characteristics reminded her strangely of her own beloved father.[12]

This woman was Helen Cadbury.

Notes

1 Alexander, Helen Cadbury and Maclean, J. Kennedy, *Charles M. Alexander: A Romance of Song and Soul-winning*, (London: Marshall, 1920), p. 18.

2 Ibid., p. 19.

3 Ibid., p. 20.

4 Ibid., p. 20.

5 The Moody Church is an independent evangelical church in Chicago.

6 'The Fundamentals' (or its full title is, 'The Fundamentals: A Testimony to the Truth') was originally a collection of ninety articles published quarterly by the Testimony Publishing Company of Chicago in twelve volumes between 1910–1915. Later it was republished by the Bible Institute of Los Angeles into four volumes. It attempted to clearly state the fundamentals of the Christian faith to oppose the biblical *higher criticism* of the time. A. C. Dixon was one of the editors.

7 See more of his biographical information later on pp. 173–75 in this book.

8 See more of his biographical information later on pp. 225–226 in this book.

9 Davis, George T. B., *Torrey and Alexander: The study of World-wide revival*, (New York: Fleming Revell, 1905).

10 The Glory Song—words and music were written by C. H. Gabriel

11 Ibid., p. 80.

12 Ibid., p. 80.

7 The romance of Helen and Charles

Helen had felt her loneliness but she was attracted to Charles and, behind the scenes, Charles himself had also felt the loneliness of his life, wanting to find a woman who could be his wife. Later, he shared more fully the story of his romance with Helen, which was recorded in the Sunday Strand:

It is true, [he wrote] that for years I had longed for a wife who could go with me into all kinds of society, and who would love the poor, the drunkard, and those who were away down in sin; a soul-winner and a real help-meet. I had reserved in my mind to choose my wife, and had decided that she must have this and the other qualities of mind and heart, but had never been able to find one that combined all the desired qualifications. During the Christmas season of 1903, which I was spending alone in London, I surrendered the whole matter to God, never dreaming that his answer would come so quickly, or that Birmingham would be the place where I should find my wife. During an afternoon meeting in Bingley Hall a week or two later, I noticed a young lady upon one of the platform seats. Immediately a feeling came over me that there was the answer to prayer. I did not know who she was, but observed her closely, and grew to love her, for I saw that she went after the salvation of souls. I noticed that in the after-meetings she usually went to the back of the Hall, and was not afraid to stay late, and work long and earnestly, sometimes with the most wretched-looking and poorly-clad women and girls. The more I saw of her the more thoroughly I was convinced that, as far as I was concerned, she was my choice, though I was still asking the Lord constantly to take everything into his hands.

I had noticed a silver-haired lady with her, evidently her mother. One day early in the mission, this lady gave me an invitation to spend my rest-day at her home. I accepted, and after she had gone, I turned to someone and asked who the lady was. 'Why that is Mrs Richard Cadbury,'... I was surprised, as I had already visited the home of some of her relatives. It was not until the last rest-day of the mission that I, with several others of the mission staff, was entertained at Uffculme. Strangely enough, and quite unknown to each other until afterwards, my future wife and I were praying earnestly on that same Friday night for the Lord's guidance in this matter. Each of us had a hard battle to fight in our own self-will, but each finally surrendered to the Lord, to have, or not to have, as He should will.[1]

Charles had had many lonely times and experiences when travelling from place to place in his own country or abroad and had longed for the companionship of a wife and a home to call their own. He was willing to wait for the right person rather than make a wrong decision. Writing of Charles McCallon Alexander, and the dangers of loneliness, and making wrong choices of a wife, J. Kennedy Maclean wrote:

Those are perilous moods ... and they may easily prove to be a man's undoing unless he is firmly convinced that God is ordering his life. Without the safe anchorage, shipwreck is inevitable, for the public man of charm and personality is always open to flattering attentions and under their influence he may choose one way when God is inviting him to walk another.... In spite of a multitude of friends and of a heart-hunger for one upon whom he might lavish the wealth of his great love, he held himself under a control, which was possible only to one whom nothing but the highest would satisfy.[2]

Two days after the mission, on another visit to Uffculme, Charles proposed to Helen, who accepted. Charles was due to meet up with the rest of the evangelistic party in the Cadbury's country retreat at Wynd's Point in the Malvern Hills, but he remained at Uffculme and sent a message to Torrey and the team. Mrs Emma Cadbury, unknown to her at the time, was the instigator of the romance between Helen and Charles, yet this would bring a different life not only for Helen but for herself. Daisy and Beatrice were due to be returning home after their educational studies and Beatrice would be a suitable companion as a replacement for Helen (Daisy would be married soon after Helen). However, right now Daisy was abroad, and Beatrice was at college in London. Emma was selfless in that she wanted the best for Helen, but she was also aware that it would mean she would lose her loving daughter's companionship, not only in the home but in her charitable work. Emma had been drawn to Charles Alexander as a suitable husband for Helen from the beginning and she thought he reminded her of her own dear husband. Since Richard's death five years beforehand, Helen and Emma had been bound together in a very special way.

> The love for her parents had been the controlling passion of Helen's life. The protection of and fellowship with her beloved mother had been a sacred trust and constant joy, and nothing but the gift which God had now bestowed upon her would have ever drawn her from her mother's side.[3]

This was a whirlwind romance, and the engagement was

announced. Many messages of congratulations were sent. Torrey, on receiving the news, wrote, 'I am glad of the news. I am sure you can do better work married, but I have never before met anyone whom I would have been glad to see you marry.'[4]

They spent the ten days of their engagement together at Uffculme before Charles set off for his Irish campaign. It was during this time that they shared their life history and Helen confessed her previous lack of trust in the Scriptures. Charles wanted to support her in her assurance of them.

Charles had not only fallen with love with Helen, but he had also developed a strong bond with her mother, Emma, and had realized the sacrifice that Emma would be making in releasing Helen so that she could marry him. Charles was very grateful for Emma's unselfishness and, soon after he left Uffculme, he wrote a short note to Emma with his grateful thanks for the permission to marry Helen:

> Addressed to Mrs Emma R Cadbury
> Uffculme
> 1904
> From
> Charles M Alexander
> Russell's Hotel, Dublin
> My Gentle English Mother,
>
> Your kind sweet face comes before me almost as often as does Helen's and that is continually. The joy bells are still ringing in my heart not so wildly as they did that night I knew but they are ringing more steadily with a mellow cadence that thrills my inmost soul. Do I need to thank you on paper to make you understand my gratitude for the great treasure you have given me?

If you are not getting better please secure a good doctor.

If there is any advice at any time speak freely and I shall be glad.

The feeling in the meetings here is quite remarkable. On Wednesday night the fourth night, ninety people confessed Christ. So early in the series and from an audience of 2700 it was glorious.

I am praying for you and love you,

Charles

Friday[5]

Both Charles and Helen recognized that, in each other, God had answered their prayers in providing a lifelong partner. Soon after departing Charles reiterated this unexpected provision by God and, referring to Helen in a short note as my 'Answer to Prayer', he wrote the following:

Helen, Emma, Beatrice and Daisy, 1904

My dear 'Answer to Prayer',

You seem to almost have a halo about you as I think of you as an answer to a call from on high.

We have stopped for ten minutes and we shall soon be on the ship.

I have just received this letter which will explain itself. You can see I must go immediately to work.

I sent you a note. By the watchman which you have received but I wanted to talk to you a little more for I shall be so tangled in committees.

I am sure you will feel neglected when the work begins. You will have to take me as I am.

I wish I had more time to be good to you.

All things work together for good to them that love God. Whatever comes is one of the 'all things'.

I have just been thinking that the best way to prepare to make you happy is to be helpful and kind to those who need me where I am.

Lovingly,

Charles

Saturday

Revelations 3:12[6]

During their time apart, Helen looked forward to receiving Charles' letters and spent each day writing to him, but it was hard to bear this separation after such a short time of being together.

Charles wrote the following to her soon after leaving:

'I have you in my heart' (Phil 1.7).

My Darling,

I have just seen the last wave of thy dear hand and one last look at a Bonny head that in a few days has won my heart.

Canaan is a fair country.

God will keep this new union and I feel sure His Spirit led you to quote the verse 'Perfect love casteth out fear' your sweet voice is still ringing in my ears.

Thy gentle mother gave me the very one I needed on top of the other.

I have a number of hard questions to settle in the next few days pray for me that they may be settled for the best interests of our King.

The nearer we get to Christ the nearer we are to each other.

Lovingly and unconditionally,

Charles[7]

This letter reflects the spiritual bond, which was to be their foundation in married life, of being close to Christ and thereby closer to each other. It also conveys Charles' affection with references of his heart being won by her. He refers to her as having a bonny head and the pleasure he had in being given permission by Helen's mother to marry Helen as well as recognizing that he needed her. This love would continue throughout their married life and would fulfil one of his mottos: 'Only one day at a time to live, only one person to please,'[8] referring to his Saviour which would then reflect in his love for Helen.

Helen made use of her time in writing the biography of her father, Richard Cadbury, as she knew her future married life would be busy and full of travelling, and not conducive to this work. Charles, in his letters, sends some suggestions of biographies to read that would assist her in her writing. Charles was not only thoughtful but practical in these matters. He could not return to Helen until the end of June, having undertaken campaigns in Ireland, Bristol, Bradford and Brighton. However, before he departed, he ensured that his photographer friend Reginald Haines had taken photographs of Helen and Uffculme so that he could take some reminders with him on his tours. Messages of congratulations flooded Uffculme and to Charles on his tours. Charles, while on his tours, wrote letters to Helen; these show his strong affection for her, which had developed in such a short time. A quick visit by Helen, her mother and her younger sister was made to Bristol to see Charles at his meetings, where afterward they caught a few hours together. Then Helen, with these family members, was rushing off to Rome to visit her sister, Daisy, who would return home with them for the wedding. While in Rome, Helen was greeted with a message from Charles for her arrival. It said:

> Seems like a tear stays in my eye
> Since you went away.[9]

Charles was able to fit in a short visit on one of his rest-days. On the Friday he was able to stay at Uffculme, if he was back on the early train on Saturday morning to return to Bradford. He looked forward to meeting Helen's sister, Daisy, for the first time.

During their times of correspondence, Charles tackled the subject of *higher criticism* and the inerrancy of the Bible, as Helen had been influenced by the teachings of *higher criticism*. Charles sent her books to read on the matter and was willing in his correspondence to confirm the authority and inerrancy of the Bible. It was during this time that Helen began to reaffirm her submission to the authority of the Bible, as well as giving her intellectual difficulties to her Saviour. In another short visit to Uffculme, Charles was able to challenge Daisy about her own personal standing with God as she had never made a personal profession of faith. On a short few days' visit to Brighton, to the Torrey-Alexander mission at the Dome, Daisy made her own personal declaration of saving faith in Christ at the end of one of the meetings where Torrey preached.

Notes

1 Ibid., pp. 80, 81.

2 Maclean, John Kennedy; *'When Home Is Heaven.' A Brief Sketch of the Home-Life of Mr & Mrs Charles M. Alexander*, (London: Marshall Brothers Ltd., 1922), p. 6, 7.

3 Alexander, Helen Cadbury and Maclean, J Kennedy, *Charles M. Alexander: A*

Romance of Song and Soul-winning, p. 82.

4 Fox, Simon, *Helen Cadbury and Charles M Alexander, A love that embraced the world*, (London: Marshall Morgan and Scott Publications, 1989), p. 40.

5 Friday but no other specific date, 1904. Undated but the occasion means it is 1904—with kind permission of N. Bradley, Helen's great nephew.

6 Saturday but no other specific date, 1904. Personal papers, with the kind permission of N. Bradley, Helen's great nephew.

7 Undated but the occasion means it is 1904, Personal papers, with the kind permission of N. Bradley, Helen's great nephew.

8 'I will never forget her first husband's life motto: "Only one day at a time to live, only one person to please!"' In the book: Samuel, Leith, *A Man under Authority, LEITH SAMUEL, The autobiography,* (Reading, Berks, UK: Christian Focus Publications, 1993), p. 46.

9 Alexander, Helen Cadbury and Maclean, J Kennedy, *Charles M. Alexander: A Romance of Song and Soul-winning*, p. 89.

8 The wedding and honeymoon of Helen and Charles

Wedding plans had been made for Thursday 14th July 1904. Helen and Charles were able to spend the first two weeks of July together and to finalize their plans. Helen, being a Quaker, was to be married according to Quaker tradition which included no flowers in the 'Friends' Meeting House' where the ceremony would take place. Many guests were unfamiliar with the Quaker's wedding customs, which had no formal order of service and would have times of silent prayer. Helen was escorted by her brother, Barrow, and the eight bridesmaids: her two sisters, Daisy and Beatrice; five nieces or cousins; and Torrey's daughter, Blanche. Both Helen and Charles made declarations before God and in the presence of the 'Friends' (i.e., the Quakers) and guests, of their love for each other and in becoming husband and wife. There were some public prayers and reading of the Bible and some words of encouragement before the signing of the marriage certificate. The ring that was given to her by Charles had engraved on the inside the words, 'Each for the other, and both for God', which became their family motto. This motto was also displayed on a frame and, later, was displayed in their home. There was a large guest list but unfortunately, even though there were guests and friends from the USA, Charles' immediate family were unable to attend. A large reception was held in in the grounds of Uffculme. That night they spent their honeymoon at the Cadbury's retreat at Wynd's Point, in the Malvern Hills and they had the following day together before returning to Uffculme.

Helen had successfully applied for American citizenship; at this time, you could not hold dual nationality in America, so she relinquished her British citizenship. Then they set off on Saturday for Liverpool to board SS Lucania for America, arriving in New York on 23rd July. Even on their voyage across the Atlantic they used the opportunity for song and sharing the gospel with the passengers. A programme of entertainment showed the following:

In aid of the
Seaman's Charities of Liverpool and New York
Held on board the
Cunard Royal Mail Steamship 'Lucania'
Captain—J.B. Watt
Thursday, July 21st, 1904, at 8.30 p.m.
(Various items including:)
Song: 'When the nights are dreary'—(Robert Harkness) Mr C. M. Alexander
....
Song 'Somebody' Mr C. M. Alexander
....
Accompanists
Mrs Alexander and Dr Creser.[1]

An affectionate letter from Helen to her mother, written as they were in sight of America, reflects her love for her mother and sisters but shows how she was wrapped up in her love for Charles. It also gives insight into their private devotions in reading and praying together. They were reading through the book of Acts, in the New Testament, together during the journey across the Atlantic.

Helen and Charles' wedding photo of guests
Back: Arthur Bradley, William
Standing: Richard, Miss Torrey, Dr Torrey, Charles, Helen, Daisy, Jessie,
Barrow, Thomas Clarke, Beatrice, Isabel, Arnold, Dick Butler
Seated: Emma Wilson, Caroline with David, Mrs Torrey, Emma, Victor
Clarke, Geraldine, Cherry, Emmeline with Joy, Edith with Betty
On the ground: Dorothea, Paul, Irene Clarke, Dorothy, William Butler

Friday July 22nd, 1904

My own dearest Motherie,

The evening of the last day on board has come, and we can already see in the distance a flashlight from the American shores—so I want to let you know at once that we are safely arrived at the end of the first stage of our journey. Our thoughts have been with thee and you all every day—and we love you more and more. We have been lazy about writing—and even about reading—and have just rested and had a happy time. Do rest, won't you? And take care of your dear selves—I wish you could have been with us, to see what a happy time we have been having. My dear old boy is so good to me, and we love each other better every day. I only hope I shan't grow selfish with being so lovingly looked after—I am so proud of dear old Charles—everybody loves him, passengers and crew … An old Kentuckian gentleman said to me one day, 'Your husband is the most popular man on the boat.' … We have such lovely prayer times and reading together. We are reading through Acts. My own treasure, I do think of thee so much, and often long to put my arms around thee, and give thee a loving hug—but I can't feel exactly homesick … We do both love thee with all our hearts—and I can never thank thee and Daddy enough for all you have been and are to me. Dear, sweet old Daisy and Betsy. We do love them too. Do give them a big hug from us … dear old Barrow and William wrote too. Wasn't it sweet of them … We must go and pack now. Breakfast is at 6.30 tomorrow morning—Mr Fitt is going to meet us in New York—and tell us how the journey can be mapped out. With dearest love from us both and a special hug from me,

Ever and ever thy own little

Helen.[2]

On arrival in New York, Mr A. P. Fitt[3] met them and drove them to the Netherland Hotel on Fifth Avenue, near Central Park. Helen was quickly introduced to lots of Charles friends during the day and, later in the evening, they had dinner at the hotel with Samuel H. Hadley.[4] Then, after dinner, he took them to the Hadley Hall Rescue Mission on the Bowery, where they heard many testimonies of conversions. The place reminded Helen of her reading of Sam Hadley's work in the Water Street Mission, which he recounted in his book, *Down In Water Street*, that Helen had read. Afterwards, Sam Hadley took them to a Midnight Mission and then to a restaurant in Chinatown. Eventually at one o'clock in the morning, Charles and Helen arrived back at their hotel. This was Helen's first introduction to America and what a hectic day! They visited some of Helen's relatives in Philadelphia for a couple of days and, later, they travelled to Albany where they took a buggy ride, enjoying the scenery. The next day they rode on an open trolley-car through the beautiful countryside to arrive at Northfield, the home of D. L. Moody and his family. Charles led the singing for a week at the Northfield Conference for Christian Workers and stayed at the home of the Fitts. After the conference, Helen and Charles journeyed to Niagara for a break and to enjoy the spectacular falls. Helen found time to write a postcard to her mother, showing Niagara Falls:

> Friday morning Aug 4, 1904
>
> We got into Buffalo at 7.40, changed there, and had breakfast on the train before reaching Niagara. We left Northfield yesterday about 5 o'clock—have the whole day here and travel again on the night train reaching Chicago tomorrow morning. We are having the loveliest time. Lots of love from, Helen.[5]

They travelled onto Chicago where a large reception had been arranged for them at the Moody Bible Institute; here Helen met many of Charles' friends. Having spent five days in Chicago, they journeyed to St Louis, Missouri, where the World's Fair was being held. They were able to enjoy a day at the fair before the Sunday was spent in services, where Charles joined up once again with Wilbur Chapman—Chapman speaking and Charles leading the singing. The next stage of their journey was to Knoxville, Tennessee, with the main purpose of visiting Charles' family, as well as visiting Charles' familiar haunts and many of his friends. Then came the time to prepare to leave the family, which was so hard that Homer, Charles' brother, ended up returning with them! On their return journey, they stopped off at Winona Lake Bible Conference in Indiana where they met up again with Wilbur Chapman and were able to be entertained by the well-known evangelist, Billy Sunday, and his wife. Eventually, they were on their way back to New York with Homer boarding S.S. Oceanic to cross the Atlantic and return to England.

They returned to Uffculme, receiving a warm welcome. A welcome reception was held at Uffculme by Helen's mother. They only stayed for a couple of days as Charles was holding various campaigns in England and Wales. It was while they were in Liverpool for one of the campaigns that the hosts and choir members wanted to celebrate the Alexanders' marriage. It was felt that a gift, when the city was full of poverty, was inappropriate; hence, a large wedding feast was held on January 7, 1905, where 2,300 poor and deprived members of the city celebrated the couple's marriage. After Charles' speech and gospel presentation, his wife:

> next bravely mounted the high platform and likewise expressed her
> deep gratitude for the wedding present. As she had been watching the
> people during the evening, the scene had called her back, in thought,
> to the parable of the Wedding Feast related by Christ while on earth.
> To the poor present she said, 'What we long for above everything else
> is that all who came here tonight to rejoice with us should learn to
> know and to love the dear Saviour who fills our lives so full of joy.[6]

After a whirlwind romance, the start of their married life continued in the same fashion.

Torrey and Alexander

Torrey and Alexander's work was very much a teamwork with their respective wives and they all became close friends. Mrs Torrey had travelled extensively with her husband and now Helen would become a similar worker alongside Charles. Often the wives would not be recognized publicly for their work:

> In a quiet, unostentatious way they scarcely ever come prominently before the public ... Yet both ladies are as whole-hearted as their distinguished husbands in their efforts to induce men and women to forsake sin and follow Christ.[7]

Helen was recognized by her close workers to be ardent in the after meetings and others knew that she had the necessary qualities to be a sympathetic and successful Christian worker. A story was told by Torrey that, during one meeting at the Bolton Mission, there was a destitute and distraught woman that Helen had noticed and was trying to help. The woman could not accept that God could love such a one as her and claimed that God could love someone like Helen but not her. The woman looked straight at Helen and asked her for a kiss, thinking that if Helen, a cultured lady, could show her this act of compassion, then maybe there was hope that God could love her. Helen at first shrank from this thought but with compassion she kissed her. This was a real practical demonstration of Helen's ability and concern to show others the love of Christ through her. At the following meetings, this woman attended but now she was neat, clean and tidy, reflecting her new nature within. Both Mrs Torrey and Helen were the 'truest of helpmeets'[8] to their husbands.

Married life was going to be hectic and full of travelling. From February to July 1905, the London Campaign was successful with thousands attending the meetings and the Royal Albert Hall was full to overflowing with crowds queuing outside. Helen and Charles decided to rent accommodation in Gloucester Road to have some time together in London and while a new family home was being built for them in Birmingham. Helen's mother and sister were able to oversee the building of this new home, which was just a few fields away from Uffculme.

Life was filled with gruelling schedules, travel and campaigns. The summer of 1905 saw a break after the London campaigns and there was also the marriage of Daisy, Helen's sister, to Dr Neville Bradley[9] of Liverpool to celebrate. Daisy had met Neville the previous year at Helen's and Charles' wedding. It was at this time that the building of 'Tennessee' was completed and, with its furniture in, they were able to spend just one night in it before they were off again to America.

'Tennessee'—their English home

Charles and Helen decided to call their home 'Tennessee' after Charles' American home state. 'Tennessee' was their real home and base in spite of their many journeys abroad.

> The simple home[10] which Mr and Mrs Alexander built on the outskirts of Birmingham was situated quite close to 'Uffculme', Mrs Cadbury's home, only a road separating the two. Its lawns and gardens were a transformation from fields that had once been part of the Uffculme estate. To link it with the other home across the ocean, it was named 'Tennessee', after Mr Alexander's native state. Thus, from its earliest beginnings, 'Tennessee' bound both husband and wife together with golden chains of memory and tender associations. As the years passed by, additions and improvements were made to the house and grounds to meets its changing needs. After Mrs Cadbury's Home-going, some

'tea-sheds' which adjoined the 'Tennessee' garden, and which had been built by Mr Cadbury as shelters for summer parties for poor children and for mission picnics of all kinds, passed into the Alexander's possession. No longer usable for their original purpose without the adjoining fields, the tea-sheds were adapted to form a cosy 'den' and work-rooms for Mr Alexander. Here he had his unique hymn-book library, and stored his ever increasing collection of photographs and lantern-slides, recording his constant journeyings in the service of Christ. Many a hymn was born here, many a book and article were written, bringing 'tidings of great joy' to homes all over the world.[11]

In their home, Charles and Helen were able to reflect different aspects of their lives and service to Christ. Although Charles was used to being in the public eye with many thousands watching him, now he was able to be at home with his wife and they were able to serve others in a more personal way:

It was not enough to invite into the sanctities of his home circle those who had a place in his heart; having invited and received them, he enswathed them in a love that knew no bounds and acknowledged no limitations. To the personal comfort of his guests he devoted himself with the tenderest care, bringing wraps to shield them from imaginary draughts, removing the boots from their feet with his own hands, and bringing warm slippers to take their place, putting them into the most comfortable corners, his face glowing all the time with that infectious joy that spread like a shaft of sunlight to all within its sphere. And then, when the day was hastening to its close, he would gather his friends into the drawing-room and sing with them those delightful songs of Zion with which his name will ever be associated ... As the hour for retiring approached, he would bring the company back to the things of God, and as all dropped upon their knees he would lead them in a prayer as simple and beautiful as that of a little child. When there were children among the guests, he loved to carry them upstairs, Mrs Alexander lending her aid and tucking them in with a good-night kiss.[12]

Although home life was busy, time was made for song and music as well as time for plenty of laughter. They both had endless energy when they were well. Helen, although wealthy, was never 'snobbish' and their home was welcoming to everyone. She was a perfectionist and could be quite demanding of others to reach similar standards. She did not suffer fools gladly, yet she was loved by so many close to her. People described her as dominant but at the same time full of fun.

However, at this stage in 1905, they only enjoyed an overnight stay in their new home 'Tennessee' before setting off again for America. This time they were accompanied by Helen's mother and her sister, Beatrice, who were visiting America for the first time. In some ways Emma and Beatrice followed in some of Helen's first footsteps in America by visiting some of the mission places in New York that Helen frequented on her first visit. They also visited some of the Cadbury relatives in Philadelphia, followed by joining the company at the Christian Workers' Conference in Northfield, Massachusetts, where Charles was due to be taking meetings.

Notes

1 A programme found in personal archives, with kind permission of C. Mary Penny, Helen's great niece.

2 Dated: Friday 22nd July 1904, from the boat, RMS 'Lucania'. Personal papers, with kind permission of N. Bradley, Helen's great nephew.

3   Arthur Percy Fitt (1869–1947) was married to Moody's daughter Emma. He was D. L. Moody's personal secretary and the author of Moody's biography.

4   Samuel H. Hadley (1842–1906) who worked at the Water Street Mission for years and had written about it in the book, *Down in Water Street*, published by Fleming H. Revell Company.

5   Dated: 4th August and posted on 5th August 1904 from Niagara Falls. Personal papers with kind permission of N. Bradley, Helen's great nephew.

6   Davis, George T. B., *Twice around the World with Alexander, Prince of Gospel Singers*, (New York: Christian Herald, 1907), p. 92, 112.

7   Maclean, John Kennedy, *Torrey and Alexander: the story of their lives*, (London: S. W. Partridge, 1905), p. 155.

8   Ibid., p. 160.

9   Neville Bradley (1878–1956).

10 Although described here as a simple home, nowadays we would not consider it simple, but this is a comparative term for a home of the time and status of the Cadbury family; the house was also extended at various times.

11 Maclean, John Kennedy, *"When Home Is Heaven" A Brief Sketch of the Home-Life of Mr & Mrs Charles M. Alexander*, pp. 12–13.

12 Ibid., pp. 14–15.

9 Helen's health concerns

It was during this time in America that Helen first suffered severe abdominal pain which affected her health but, at the beginning, she made a recovery. She, along with her mother and sister, returned earlier than Charles to 'Tennessee' to prepare their new home for some of Charles' relatives who would be visiting. This time it was to be Charles' mother, his sister, Ida, and his other brother, Leo. They all spoke highly of their stay at 'Tennessee' and both grew very fond of Helen. They enjoyed England immensely and everyone they met. Once again life was busy with entertaining and work. Helen's sister, Daisy, was leaving England as her husband, Neville Bradley, who was a doctor, was going to work in China in a missionary hospital. A catalogue of missions took place for Charles: one being in Oxford where there was initially a lot of opposition to his work and especially his methods. Helen, at this time, was still ill and was unable to join him. Here is a copy of one of her letters to him:

Nov. 12, 1905

My darling,

This is being written in the hall at Uffculme. Mother, Betsy and I have just had dinner together, and the little Mother has started off to Garrison Lane to help at the Nicholson's evening Mission Meeting—I wonder how your meetings have been. Marguerite tells me the whole Christian Union are against your work. What a pity it seems. I suppose they are afraid of what the other students will think of them and haven't courage enough to face their disapproval. I am praying for you. It is plucky of the fourteen students who are helping in the Mission. I have written lots of letters since Saturday, amongst others—to Mammy and Ida, also Mrs Simpson and Daisy and Miss Simpson, and to Dr Martin—I have also dictated many. In a letter from Richard, he says how much the Worcester people are looking forward to their excursion to visit the Oxford Mission on the 23rd. Poor

'Tennessee'

Richard has not at all got over the disappointment of your not going to Worcester, so I hope they will have a good time on the 23rd. Miss Torrey's letter had already been sent on. I do hope it reached thee safely. It had been readdressed so much that I put it inside another envelope so perhaps it was not recognised as the one she wanted. I read Mr Davis's book through yesterday—it is very good indeed. Please congratulate him from me. I see the English edition had 'Bingley Hall, Birmingham' all right. Mr Clayton came up to Tennessee this morning to make arrangements for Thursday morning. The nurse is coming in on Wed evening, and it will be quite early in the morning, so I shall be all right again for my darling boy on Friday. I am going to use the oak room, as the light is better in there—I went to have lunch with Barrow and Geraldine today and stayed till four, when Geraldine drove me home. She was so loving to me. Well, goodbye, my own Beloved.

Ever thy loving wife

Helen C. A.[1]

A few more letters followed in quick succession. Obviously with Charles' concern for her physical welfare, Helen wanted to keep him up to date with her situation and to keep in contact with him over the difficult mission at Oxford:

Wednesday November 15, 1905 (10.30 p.m.)

My own Beloved,

I am writing this upstairs in our room, just before turning out the light for the night. I was so grieved to find that it was too late to post thy letter after our Gospel Temperance friends had gone, but if it is posted early in the morning, thou wilt get it during the day. There has been quite a lot to arrange to keep things going while I am upstairs, but everybody is so good and kind it makes things easy. They had a family dinner party over at Uffculme this evening, Aunt Elsie[2] and Uncle George, Jessie and ?[3], Mr and Mrs Culwick, Edith and Arnold, Cousins Sarah and Caroline Cadbury, Henry and Isabel, George and Edith, a Miss Taylor (a cousin of Aunt Elsie) and of course Mother and Betsy, also a Mr Gordon-Thompson, a friend of Neville's. I was so sorry not to be there, but we had planned our two parties on the same day quite by mistake. I helped Betsy and ?[4] arrange who should take whom into dinner and how they should be placed at table, so had a small share in it. Our Gospel temperance friends came about 5.30 and Mr Maclean soon after. The nurse came too about the same time, so I left Mr Maclean and Mr Butler to see after them, while I went to settle her in, and see what things she wanted for herself or me. We have made thy dressing room into a most cosy little bed sitting room for her. Thou wilt see it on Friday. She seems very sweet and nice. Our party had tea at six, eleven of us altogether. After tea we made a big circle in the drawing-room, and during the talk got some very good incidents. Mr Maclean is leaving by the breakfast train in the morning. Oh, before I forget. I did not write to Mr Oatts after all. I thought as he was in Birmingham it seemed too bad not to have him come here, so I thought he might just as well come and have some lunch with thee and go down to his afternoon meeting at three o' clock. I know it would be such a pleasure to him to see thee, and I expect he would like to have been here. Tatters is so sweet—he is really getting so affectionate. Well, I must be off to bed now, as we shall be?[5] early tomorrow. I am to have a cup of tea at 6.0—and it is to be soon after 8.30, so by the time thou gets this, it will be all a thing of the past, and I shall be ready in a few short hours to welcome my darling boy home.

Goodnight, Beloved. I have that text in my heart, 'When thou passest through the waters, I will be with thee.'

Ever and forever,

Thy own loving wife,

Helen.[6]

Charles managed to squeeze in a brief visit home between meetings at Oxford. Helen wrote a letter expressing her appreciation of it:

My own dear treasure,

Thy visit home has been like a refreshing sea breeze and has left a fragrance of thy presence in the room—Darling, I love thee so much and I do thank thee for all thy love and goodness to me.

It is Daisy's birthday today. I have been thinking of her. Mother came in this morning again. Nurse read aloud 'Paul of Tarsus' to me this afternoon, also how she is going to church, and Betsy has come in to spend the evening here. I have one of thy sheets on my bed. Mother has gone down to Highgate with Miss Cave. I am thinking of thee in all thy meetings...

A big hug for thee from thy ever-loving wife,

Helen[7]

Another letter written by Helen, at the end of November 1905, expresses her love for Charles and how she misses him; maybe due to her pain she speaks of her fear of not losing his love but losing him:

> 'Perfect love casteth out fear'—I know and I have no fear in my love for thee—I know thy heart will always be true and thy love unmoved but the other is true also—'you do not truly love what you do not fear to lose' and I do dread losing, never thy love, but thy sweet, lovely presence. Still I know it is right, and I know the Lord will keep us both to do His will cheerfully—He is so good to me ....[8]

She then recounts that the nurse has been reading *Glengarry Days* to her and, also, that both her mother and Betsy were coming to see her.

> A letter addressed to
> Chas M. Alexander
> Isis Boarding House,
> Iffley Road
> Oxford
> From Tennessee
> Tuesday 5.25 p.m.
> Nov 21, 1905
> My own dearest,
>
> Another day has come and gone and such a beautiful day it has been! Brilliant sunshine, blue skies, soft cold air, singing of birds, till the morning would have almost made you think it was spring instead of autumn. But the afternoon sunset was undeceiving—The great red ball of the sun set the clouds above on fire, and sank into a bed of cold grey clouds which looked heavy with snow and soon extinguished the glory—and the trees looked bare and shivering against the sky—But

we had a bright fire inside here which lit the whole room up with a warm glow. Presently tea came up—and the firelight shone on nurse's white cap and apron and lit up the sweet outline of her face. The silver tea things glittered and winked back at the fire and thy picture looked at me dimly distinct from the shadows on the wall. We have finished 'Glengarry Days' and enjoy our work and a chat in between. Mother and Betsy are coming in again tonight. Mother reads aloud (a Welsh story by Allen Raine, called 'Tom Sails') while we two work, and nurse has a little time to herself. Everybody is good and kind, and my heart is full of gratitude to the Lord, in spite of a bit of ache which is in it all the time. Another of those painful letters of detailed congratulations upon a certain imaginary event came this morning. I suppose the Lord sees it's a bit of discipline I need; it certainly is embarrassing and gives a little pang. My heart goes out to thee in loving trust. I know thou art thinking of me and praying for me, as I for thee, and it is joy to have thee so comparatively near. Nurse is just going out for a walk so is kindly taking this to post. I feel as if I've been trusting the Lord rather shabbily after all He has done for me, and I really do trust Him for the future.

Ever and ever Thy own loving wife Helen.[9]

The letter gives an insight into Helen's relationship with Charles but also the continued support of her mother and sister and her resilience in maintaining her work as much as was possible while in pain and discomfort. It is not clear what was the actual cause of Helen's ongoing pain but there is a reference to a 'painful' letter of 'detailed congratulations upon a certain imaginary event'. We can glimpse a hint that others assumed her physical problems were connected to pregnancy which, obviously, was a cause of mental anguish.

Finally, at the end of the year, Charles had a few weeks before he would return to North America. Helen did not accompany him because her pain had worsened. The doctors had advised her that she should be able to travel to join Charles by the spring, but she continued to worsen. She was determined not to have any medical intervention until her husband had returned home and they had had some time together. Charles did not return to 'Tennessee' until July 1906. He had not realized how ill she was. The plan was for them to spend two weeks together before an operation but, after five days, she had to have an emergency operation at their own home as she was too ill to travel. On top of this she developed blood poisoning. Their long separation, and the delayed treatment also, had taken a toll on her health and it was not known if she would survive. For two long weeks Helen's life hung in the balance and many prayers around the world were made for her. Her health turned a corner and Charles felt that, as her precious life had been saved, he should have some time with her for her long-needed recuperation. Charles declined the missions with Torrey and then planned a long cruise for Helen's recovery. To add to her troubles, Helen had to contend with slander about her husband and his long absence in America, with people saying that he was already married. Charles refuted this publicly in a meeting in Birmingham. Helen faced these allegations with real 'grit' and determination, despite her poor health.

Chinese visit

Due to Helen's poor health, it was suggested by the doctor that she rested and that a cruise with sea air would be good for her recuperation. As Helen's health had improved, her mother and her sister Beatrice felt that they were free to visit Helen's other younger sister, Daisy, her husband and their new baby in Pakhoi, China where her husband was a medical missionary. Accordingly, Charles and Helen decided to follow her mother and sister to visit Daisy, in Pakhoi. Knowing the kind of characters they were, Charles and Helen used the opportunities they had on the ship by speaking of Christ. They stopped off at Egypt, Ceylon, Penang, Singapore and Hong Kong and visited many missionaries at the various ports of call, before reaching China. Dr Bradley, Daisy's husband, came to meet the party before the final leg of their journey was made, to be reunited with the other members of Helen's family in Pakhoi. It was New Year's Eve and Charles recounted:

Daisy, Emma and baby in 1907, Pakhoi

> We spent New Year's Eve in that far-away place. There were only four of us in our sitting-room at the Peak Hotel—Dr Bradley, Dr Thompson, my wife and myself. I proposed that we should have a prayer-meeting that would last out the old year and into the new. We had a blessed time in prayer for about an hour; and when we rose from our knees, I suggested that we should choose a Year Verse first thing in the new year, to be our motto all through it. We easily settled upon that old verse which is so familiar to lovers of the New Testament, John 14:1: 'Let not your heart be troubled: ye believe in God, believe also in me.'

We wondered why we were led to choose this, little dreaming how precious it would become to us before our journey was finished.[10]

They met a group of lepers in Pakhoi, who had translated the Bible into Chinese over a period of eight years. They had stored the printed copies, one Bible book at a time, until the whole Bible was translated. When they came to open the stored books, they found that ants had eaten much of the paper but, undaunted, they went on to print more copies.

While in Pakhoi, the family had a picnic at a local beauty spot and Charles, who had gone on ahead on horseback with some of the family, had a fall and remained unconscious for two days. Helen spent time in prayer. After a couple more days, he recovered but with ill effects on his eyesight, so he had to wear peculiar looking spectacles. Eventually, his eyesight returned to normal. Having recovered sufficiently, but still with his peculiar spectacles, he, along with Helen and her mother and sister, Beatrice, visited Hong Kong where he had agreed to take some meetings. This was to be his first time speaking at a large mission without Torrey or some other partner. He managed to sing with Helen accompanying him, although she certainly was not the same as Robert Harkness— Charles' favoured accompanist. The songs were interspersed with his talks. Then, having said farewell to her mother and sister, who returned to Pakhoi for a time, Charles and Helen set off for Australia to continue their cruise and Helen's 'so-called' recuperation. Her journeys of recuperation seemed to have been rather busy!

Australian visit

Due to Charles' reputation from his previous campaigns in

Australia, he was soon recognized and was engaged in various meetings in different parts of the country. One of the places was Bendigo, where Charles had first met and employed Robert Harkness as a pianist. The Harkness family entertained them and, once again, Charles was engaged in meetings. Charles' and Helen's stay was to be a few days, but it ended up being four weeks of Charles taking meetings. This was supposed to be a time of rest and recuperation for Helen, yet it was very busy. Helen fully supported her husband's work:

> Despite the fact that Mrs Alexander had been brought up in the midst of comfort, she has always been used to mission work, and since her marriage has thrown herself most heartily into her husband's work, accompanying him on his tours, and doing active personal service in revival meetings night after night. So ardent a soul-winner is she that I have seen her keep the janitor waiting half an hour to turn out the lights after a meeting, while she pleaded with some poor soul to accept Christ. She believes every Christian should be a personal worker.[11]

The death of Helen's mother, Emma

In April 1907, Charles and Helen set off on their homeward journey, via Vancouver and New York. In New York, they waited to hear from her mother and sister, who were travelling with some of her nieces but, instead of the news of their safe arrival in Vancouver, a telegram reached them informing them of Emma's death. While on board the ship, there had been an accident and Helen's mother had died. During a storm, the ship had lurched and Emma had fallen and hit her head, causing concussion. She never recovered from the concussion and died that night. It was decided to bring her mother's body back to Birmingham where she would be buried in the family grave. Helen and Charles travelled back to Winnipeg to connect with her sister, Beatrice, so that they could make the journey back home together.

Emma was buried in the family grave in Lodge Hill Cemetery, Birmingham with the remains of Helen's father.

Helen, now, had the sad task of settling her mother's estate and her mother's possessions at Uffculme.[12] Uffculme was inherited by the eldest son, Barrow, who wanted it to be used for adult education, as he had a home of his own already. The house continued to be used for seven years as an adult education centre until,

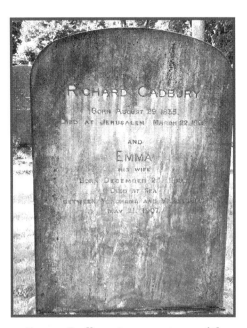

Emma Cadbury's gravestone with Richard

in 1914, it provided shelter for refugees from Belgium. In 1916, it was generously donated to the Birmingham City Council for the benefit of the people of Birmingham. It must have been a difficult task, as Helen was reminded of the many happy memories of her life there at Uffculme. It was decided that Beatrice would move into 'Tennessee' with Helen and Charles, and some of the Uffculme staff were employed by Helen at 'Tennessee'.

Chapman and Alexander

Charles, with Helen recovered, wanted to undertake more of his evangelistic missions but he could not partner with Torrey as Torrey had taken up a new role. He, therefore, teamed up with Dr Wilbur Chapman, who had asked Torrey's permission to develop this new partnership—to which Torrey agreed.

John Wilbur Chapman (1859–1918), normally referred to as Wilbur Chapman, was born in Indiana, USA. Both his parents, being Christians, had a great influence upon his life but, when he was thirteen, his mother died and his older sister became the surrogate mother to the family for a time. Although he could not put a time to his conversion, when he was seventeen, he was challenged by D. L. Moody about his spiritual state and for the first time publicly confessed Christ. He confessed to Moody that he had waivered in the assurance of salvation, but he realized, in discussion with him, that assurance is based on trust in the promises of the Scriptures. On another occasion, F. B. Meyer spoke about giving all to Christ and Chapman claimed that, from then on, he would live for Christ.

He was one of the best educated evangelists of the time, having graduated at Lake Forest University and then trained at Lane Seminary, Cincinnati. Later, he was awarded a D.D. (Doctor of Divinity) by the University of Wooster and an LL. D. (Doctor of Law) by Heidelberg University. Six days after his graduation, he married Irene E. Steddom (1860–1886),[13] whom he had known from his childhood. Soon after this, he took his first pastorate, pastoring two churches: one in Liberty, Indiana; and the other at College Corner, Ohio. He became a pastor to many churches during his lifetime.

After four years of marriage, a baby girl, Bertha Irene, was born to them but, within the month, Mrs Chapman died leaving Wilbur devastated at the loss of his wife and Bertha Irene without a mother. Two years later, Wilbur married Agnes Pruyn Strain and they had four children. He found that his true passion was as an evangelist and he set about various campaigns and eventually partnered with Charles Alexander. Chapman wrote books as well as hymns—his best-known hymn being, 'One day when heaven was filled with his praises'. 'Out of the ivory palaces' was a sermon Chapman preached and Henry Barraclough (1891–1983)[14] based his well-known hymn on it. He was an advocate of Bible teaching conferences and became the leader of the Winona Lake Conference, and developed the conferences at Montreat, North Carolina, and Stony Brook, Long Island, New York. At one point, he was the Vice President of the Moody Bible Institute and D. L. Moody himself recognized Chapman as the best evangelist in America. In 1910, he remarried, after the death of his second wife—this time to Mabel Cornelia Moulton. He suffered ill health in his later years and died after a gallstone operation in 1918.

Pocket Testament League

Charles Alexander, while undertaking these Chapman-Alexander missions, realized afresh the importance of the Bible and people reading it for themselves. Subsequently, in discussion with Helen, they decided to reinstate and promote the Pocket Testament League (PTL). George T. B. Davis, an American friend, helped in its initial start—later he became the International Secretary of PTL. Davis had himself introduced in Philadelphia the 'Testament Circles', whereby people would carry a New Testament with them to be able to witness to people about the gospel truths. George T. B. Davis became known as 'George Take-a-Book Davis' to fit in with his initials! George had been a newspaper writer in Chicago and had previously gone to England to cover the Torrey-Alexander meetings for American and English papers.

In January 1908, Charles and Helen set off for America to undertake various campaigns and conferences and, at these, he promoted the Pocket Testament League (PTL).[15] It was not just Charles but Helen herself who told of her story of the Pocket Testament League. She spoke and challenged others to enlist in the league promising to carry the New Testament, or at least a portion of the Scriptures, with them and read the Bible daily.

> In the summer of 1908, at the Winona Bible Conference, conducted by Dr Chapman, the origin of the Pocket Testament League was related by Mrs. Alexander to a large audience of evangelists, ministers, missionaries and Christian workers. At the conclusion of the service, cards of membership were passed, and Gipsy Smith, the well-known evangelist, who was seated on the platform, was the first to join the movement. Rev. W. H. Hubbard, D.D., of Auburn, New York, was so interested that he said he wanted to purchase hundreds of Testaments for the prisoners in the State penitentiary there. Later Dr Hubbard gave Testaments to five hundred students in Berea College, Kentucky, who joined the League.[16]

Robert Harkness—Charles' Australian pianist, composer and hymnwriter—and Fred P. Morris, another Australian hymnwriter, both wrote hymns for the Pocket Testament League. The hymn, 'Carry your Bible',[17] which was dedicated to the Alexanders. They also wrote another hymn, 'Win Someone',[18] which was the other aim of the League. Robert Harkness wrote the words and music for, 'Hide God's Word in your heart',[19] which he dedicated to Mrs E. A. R. Davis, the mother of George T. B. Davis.

'Carry your Bible'

Carry your Bible with you,
Let all its blessings outflow;
It will supply you each moment,
Take it wherever you go.

Take it wherever you go,
Take it wherever you go,
God's message of love,
Sent down from above,
O take it wherever you go.

Carry the word of pardon,
Sweeter each day it will grow;
Somewhere some heart will be waiting,
Take it wherever you go.

Carry the wondrous story,
Tell it to hearts plunged in woe;
This word of gracious redemption,
Take it wherever you go.

Carry the word of promise;
Sinners unpardoned may know
God's path from sin unto safety,
Take it wherever you go.

'Win Someone'

Will you not try to win someone?
Back from the path of sin?
Telling the love of Jesus,
Will you not now begin?

Will you not try to win someone?
Someone has gone astray.
Will you not try to win someone
Back to the narrow way?

Will you not try to win someone?
Just by a word or smile?
Lifting your heart to Jesus
Praying for grace the while.

Will you not try to win someone?
Just for the Saviour's sake?
Bearing in mind His sorrow,
Knowing His heart must ache.

Will you not try to win someone?
Great is the need today.
Someone is perishing near you,
There must be no delay.

'Hide God's Word in your heart'

Hide God's Word in your heart,
Its precious Truth believe;

At His command
Take from His hand,
The Bread of Life receive.

Hide God's Word in your heart,
Hide God's word in your heart,
His Word of Love
Sent from above,
Hide God's Word in your heart.

Hide God's Word in your heart,
If you grow in grace,
And like Him be
Until you see
Your Master face to face

Hide God's Word in your heart,
And seek the Spirit's power
To understand
Each blest command
He gives from hour to hour.

Hide God's Word in your heart,
And having hidden well,
Seek out the lost,
The tempest-tossed,
Go forth His love to tell.

Hide God's Word in your heart,
Each day a verse repeat;

Tho' sin allure
Success is sure,
You cannot have defeat.

Another hymn, 'Give Time to Work for Jesus',[20] by Harkness, was also associated with the PTL work:

Give time to work for Jesus,
The Way of Life to show
To those you meet upon the street,
Let them the Gospel know.

Give time to work for Jesus,
Give time to Him each day;
Let others know, where'er you go,
Salvation's wondrous way.

Give time to work for Jesus,
And seek God's will to know;
Be much in prayer that you may bear
Rich blessings as you go.

Give time to work for Jesus,
And take God's Word as guide;
Its message learn, its truth discern,
Its promises abide.

Give time to work for Jesus,
The Lord your work will own;
Each soul you win from paths of sin
Adds glory to your crown.

On another occasion Helen shared her story of the Pocket Testament League:

> Dr H H Lowry, of the Peking University, arranged for the presentation of the League to the students; Mr. Alexander taught them the League hymn, 'Carry Your Bible' Mrs. Alexander told how the plan had been originated, and when an opportunity was given to the students to join, almost all who were present readily enlisted. Following our departure from the city, the League was vigorously promoted throughout Northern China by Mr. Cheng Ching-yi, who made one of the most brilliant seven-minute addresses at the recent World-Missionary Conference at Edinburgh and was appointed a member of the Continuation Committee of the Conference.
>
> The last place where the League was presented in China was in some respects the most interesting. It was to the scholars in the China Inland Mission School for missionaries' children at Chefoo. Under Mr. Alexander's direction the children quickly learned the League hymn, and Mrs. Alexander and others explained the aim and objects of the movement. There were nearly three hundred children present, who came from homes, not only in China but in other Eastern lands. Practically everyone who was present, including a number of missionaries, signified their desire to read and carry God's Word daily, and later on some special Testaments were sent to the children. Letters have since been received from the principal of the school telling how delighted the children were at receiving their gifts.[21]

American visits

During the year of 1908, Charles visited America six times. Helen was with him for most of these tours, having regained her energy and strength; although, in early 1909, she took a holiday with her sister Betsy to the Isle of Wight. Her letter talks of the journey and the scenery and how her health has improved with the air. There is a sweet reference to a gift which Charles had sent her:

> I must thank thee for my lovely new gold expanding bracelet for my wrist watch. It came just before we left home. Thank thee so much. It is simply lovely and will be so useful as well as pretty on our long travels. Bend thy head, and let me give thee a big hug for it. Thank thee, thank thee, Beloved. Thy own loving wife, Helen.[22]

The bracelet was a thoughtful and kind expression of his love and affection for her, especially during their times of separation.

Another Australasian mission

There was preparation for a third Australasian campaign for 1909. Life was hectic for Helen, but she seemed to have no trouble keeping up with this busy life of travel and missions. A couple of days prior to their embarkation to Australasia, Charles managed to arrange for a printing press to be delivered aboard the S. S. Makura. He had the idea of printing a daily newspaper for the passengers, which would also include in it an article by Chapman and a hymn and story by Charles, with the Pocket Testament League also being promoted. The whole party, with help from others, were involved in its production and distribution and hence, the *Makura Herald* came into existence. This resulted in many joining the PTL.

Charles loved to use opportunities in the promotion of the gospel through literature and this included seeking to get editors of newspapers to give him columns in which to write. These columns would include the words of hymns and his stories; he was ever seeking to reach people with the gospel. On one occasion with a newspaper editor, he agreed that his wife would write a daily article for the paper for the three weeks duration of the campaign! But he had not consulted with Helen first! Duly, Helen undertook the task, although she did have a sleepless night as a result. Charles' comment was that 'she would rise to a dire necessity'.[23] Sydney, Melbourne, Brisbane, Queensland and New South Wales hosted a succession of meetings with thousands in attendance.

A catalogue of tours followed to various parts of the East: China, Korea, Philippines and Japan, where thousands attended the evangelistic mission meetings and where many professed conversion. On all these occasions, the PLT was promoted with the daily reading of the Bible and for Christians to be soul winners. In China it was renamed the *Sleeve Testament League* as the Chinese kept their New Testaments in their sleeves. Thus, in April 1910, having returned via North America and various missions there, the Alexanders arrived back at 'Tennessee'—no wonder a biography of Charles Alexander is called, *Twice around the World*.[24]

Hymnals

When 'Tennessee' was purchased, there were large grounds but, on the death of Helen's mother and the loss of 'Uffculme', the old 'Tea-sheds' were incorporated into the grounds of 'Tennessee'. These 'tea-sheds' were adapted by the Alexanders into distinct areas; the first was 'The Den' and the other 'the West Room'. These rooms were a hive of industry with the Alexanders and their helpers, working on hymns, hymnals and other material. The rooms housed a large personal collection of books, hymn books, memorabilia, photographs, 'lantern slides',[25] photographic equipment,

Testaments and leaflets, as well as the well-used typewriters and printing blocks and, of course, a piano. One part of the rooms was a dedicated dark room for the photographic processing and the storage of the photographic plates. Charles loved photography and he always made use of it where he could in the promotion of the gospel, especially the production of souvenirs from the campaigns and the newspaper publications. These 'Tea-sheds' were a hub for the production of hymns, not only in hymn writing but in their production into print. Dr W. H. Fitchett of Melbourne in 1911 visited 'Tennessee' and wrote:

> The process of evolving a Gospel hymn-book is by no means so simple as some persons imagine. It is an art that requires expert skill, and it needs money, much money. Mr Alexander has brought both science and art to the process, and he has spent with a most unselfish spirit much money upon it. Copyrights, even of hymn tunes, are properly fenced round with legal guards. They must be bought before they can be used ... The whole profits on these hymn-books are expended in maintaining and carrying on evangelistic work, and not for private purposes. Mr Alexander's home in Moor Green Lane is really a little colony of workers.[26]

Many, many hymn books were produced by the Alexanders, some of them under the name Alexander, e.g., *Alexander Hymns* 1-4, *Alexander's Gospel Songs* but, also, others such as *Immanuel's Praise* and *Work and Worship*.

Alongside the hymn books, many hymn sheets for the campaigns were produced. This was a huge work which involved not only Charles and Helen but a team of workers. At one time the 'plates'[27] of the new hymn book, *Alexander's Male Choir,* were not finished when Charles and Helen departed for Australia. So, Mr F, S, Turney, who had been involved in the technical production side of the hymn book, set sail on the next boat to take the plates out to Australia—so important was the need of the printed words and music.

In the 'Tea-sheds', the work of hymn writing and composing was done alongside the compilation of new hymn books and the work entailed in the copyrighting of the lyrics and tunes. Helen would work alongside this group of men and was involved in the copyrighting process. When she was not there, her photograph on the table in the middle of the room was a reminder of her to Charles. Alongside the work on the hymn books, Helen wrote two hymns: 'After the shadows have passed away,' and There's a city bright and fair,' but she also arranged some of the choir pieces and was known to adapt or add verses to existing hymns.[28] Looking at the hymns she added to or arranged, it seems that there were consistent themes which she either wanted to re-enforce, as they already existed in the hymn, or to add additional material to emphasize important content. The themes consisted of the gospel call and appeal, with the Saviour calling sinners to himself and his redemptive work for them with a gospel pardon. On the other side of the coin, her hymns were exhorting Christians to be obedient to the commands of Christ and pleading for them to preach the gospel —heaven and glory also appear in her words. Helen continued in the work of hymns and hymn books, updating copyrights until quite late in her life.

'Kentucky'

Charles and Helen introduced a new initiative as an outcome of all this work and the facilities by inviting a group of male assistants to help in the production of the hymn books. At first Charles and Helen entertained them at 'Tennessee' but it was felt that they, the 'boys', as Charles referred to them, needed to have their own 'home'. A nearby house was rented for these young men, who were mainly American and Australian and it was named 'Kentucky', after the neighbouring state to Tennessee in America. These men were known as the 'Kentuckians'. They were still regular visitors to 'Tennessee', joining the family each day for Bible reading and prayer followed by breakfast before they set to work, but they were able to have their own 'home'.

Notes

1 November 12, 1905. Personal papers, with the kind permission of N. Bradley, Helen's great nephew.

2 Elizabeth Mary Cadbury (1858–1951) was known as Elsie and was George Cadbury's wife.

3 The handwriting is difficult to read, especially as the name may be a 'pet name', but I presume it is Rev. Thomas G. Clarke (1853–1922), Jessie's husband; Jessie being Helen's elder half-sister.

4 The handwriting is difficult to read. I presume it was one of the servants.

5 The handwriting is difficult to read but the sense it not altered.

6 November 15, 1905. Personal papers, with the kind permission of N. Bradley, Helen's great nephew.

7 November 19, 1905. Personal papers, with the kind permission of N. Bradley, Helen's great nephew.

8 November 20, 1905. Personal papers, with the kind permission of N. Bradley, Helen's great nephew.

9 Personal papers, with the kind permission of N. Bradley, Helen Cadbury's great nephew.

10 Davis, George T. B., *Twice around the World with Alexander, Prince of Gospel Singers*, p. 315.

11 Ibid., p. 90.

12 From 1907, Uffculme was used for adult education, which had been Richard Cadbury's initiative, but, eventually, Uffculme — the house and its thirty-six acres of land — was donated to Birmingham City Council for the benefit of its people.

13 In many accounts it has been spelt as Steddon but, in the biography written by his close friend and a cousin, Chapman's wife's maiden name is spelt as Steddom: Ford C. Ottman, *J. Wilbur Chapman, A biography*, (Garden City, New York: Doubleday, 1920), pp. 39, 57.

14 Henry Barraclough (1891–1983) was born in York, England, and was a talented organist and pianist. At the age of twenty-three, he joined Alexander as his pianist. In 1917, he volunteered to be drafted for the British forces for the war. From 1919–1961, he worked for the General Assembly of the Presbyterian Church where he was secretary and then administrator. He wrote about 20 hymns and 120 tunes. His most famous hymn was the 'Ivory Palaces'.

15 The Pocket Testament League (PTL) is now also known as Bridge Builders.

16 Davis, George, T. B., *The Pocket Testament League Around the World*, Philadelphia: The Pocket Testament League, 1910, pp. 25–26.

17 Ibid., p. 91.

18 Ibid., p. 93.

19 Ibid., p. 92.

20 Ibid., p. 87 & hymn text inserted between pp. 82 & 83.

21 Ibid., p. 56

22 Feb 15, 1909. Personal papers with kind permission of N. Bradley, Helen's great nephew.

23 Alexander, Helen Cadbury and Maclean, J Kennedy, *Charles M. Alexander: A Romance of Song and Soul-winning*, p. 149.

24 Davis, George T. B., *Twice around the World with Alexander, Prince of Gospel Singers*.

25 Lantern slide is a positive print of a photograph on a glass slide; sometimes the glass was hand-coloured to enhance its appeal.

26 Alexander, Helen Cadbury and Maclean, J Kennedy, *Charles M. Alexander: A Romance of Song and Soul-winning*, p. 180.

27 'Plates': printing plates were used at this time for transferring images onto a metal sheet so that it could be printed. This was needed because of the production of the musical score.

28 The hymn, 'All unseen the master walketh': its author, Thomas MacKellar, in *Alexander's Gospel Songs No. 2.* Verse two was written by Helen Alexander, i.e., 'When thy loved ones', with Helen making the original verse two into a refrain. She also arranged the music for it in *Alexander's Male Choir, the English edition.* The hymn, 'Jesus is our Captain' (sometimes changed to, 'Jesus is our Leader'), written by Mary Bernstecher, with Helen adding stanzas and adapting it, in *Alexander's Hymns No. 3.* Helen Alexander and Carrie Breck (nee Ellis), also known as Mrs. Frank Breck, wrote, 'There's a city bright and fair', in *Alexander's Male Choir.* W. E. Witter wrote, 'While Jesus whispers to you', with Helen Alexander adding verses 3 and 4 in *Alexander's Gospel Songs No. 2.* "Work for the night is coming', was written by Annie Louisa (nee Walker), also known as Mrs. Harry Coghill, with Helen Alexander writing verse 3 in *Alexander's Hymns No. 4.*

10 Trials of life

Charles' health issues

Charles' and Helen's time back at 'Tennessee' was short lived, as Charles had a mission in Cardiff from April–May,1910. Straight after this, Charles sailed for America, this time without Helen, as it was going to be a short visit. Charles, while in America, was taken seriously ill with appendicitis. He recovered sufficiently to return home but they were soon busy again, with Charles attending a conference in early June in Edinburgh.

With a constant stream of visitors from all over the world visiting them at 'Tennessee', they decided to have a short break in Cornwall—one of their favourite places. Then, they were scheduled to spend summer at 'Tennessee' but, in July, Charles' health deteriorated with appendicitis and he had to have an operation to remove the appendix, which was performed at their home. Charles had written a note to Helen before the operation and left her to open it while undergoing the surgery. He wrote:

> My precious Helen, I love you and I can never tell you the hundred thousand ways you help and make me … It is heaven to live with you. You are my best adviser. When I think of you, honey,[1] I always think of the Scripture verse, 'Exceedingly abundantly above all that we can ask or think.' You have made it so easy to approach this solemn event.[2]

Even during his time of convalescence, they both witnessed to the medical staff and the many visitors and gave out their PTL gospels. They squeezed in another two weeks holiday in Cornwall to aid his recovery and then returned to their busy lives with entertaining and sharing the gospel. In their living room they had a motto on display, 'Each for the other and both for God', and this motto they lived out in their public and private lives. Charles worked hard on his hymn books and hymns and was often surrounded by his assistants, working with him on these projects during this summer.

In September 1910, after Charles' full recovery, there was once again a stream of visitors to 'Tennessee', including ones from Australia but, also, his long-standing friend and co-worker, Wilbur Chapman, arrived with his new bride. Once again Charles and Chapman were able to arrange some evangelistic meetings in different British cities, before all of them—Charles, Helen, Dr and Mrs Chapman—set sail once again for New York in early October, not returning to England until March 1911. Charles had made a remarkable recovery!

Birth and death

By late 1910, Helen was pregnant. She had longed to be a mother and they both rejoiced in this news but that did not stop the busyness of travel and campaigns. At the beginning of June 1911, Helen went into labour, which proved to be a very difficult one, but eventually a baby boy was born. He survived for only a short time and died at their home at 'Tennessee'. Helen's first words, having learnt the news, was, 'The Lord gave and the Lord hath taken away. Blessed be the name of the Lord.'[3] She took some time to physically recover from the difficult labour and, although there seemed to be no medical reason why she could not conceive again, she never did and it was a great sadness to them both. But 'husband and wife learned to walk more humbly before their God, bound to each other

The gravestone of Helen's baby with the inscription: 'June 30th 1911, Infant son of Charles McCallon and Helen Cadbury Alexander, "Blessed be the name of the Lord"'

in a new bond of tender sympathy and love that drew them nearer to God.'[4] In many ways their home was a reflection of her parents' home—a place of hospitality and service—but it was never to be her like her parents' home in being full of their own children. They did, however, often end up with various members of their family's children, often being semi-adopted, and in this respect, it was like her parents' home with lots of fun for the children.

Family deaths

Two more family deaths occurred with the deaths of Charles' sister-in-law—the wife of his brother, Homer—leaving two little girls, and, secondly, the death of Helen's ten-year-old nephew, Arthur—the son of her brother, Richard. Arthur died in an accident at school but, in his pocket, was found the Pocket Testament which had been given him by his Uncle Charles and Aunt Helen, as he had joined the Pocket Testament League. Charles' and Helen's attitude seemed to be one of, 'the Lord has given and the Lord has taken away,' but that did not mean they did not experience that great sorrow that death brings and, also for them, the sorrow of childlessness. Helen, once again, showed her resilience and her ability to trust in her Saviour.

Beatrice's (Betsy) marriage

In the autumn months of 1911, Charles and Dr Chapman held missions in Northern Ireland. Helen, at the time of the Irish campaign, was only able to be there for a few days as her youngest sister, Beatrice, was going to be married and Helen was busy making all the arrangements. In a note written to Helen from Charles on her return home to 'Tennessee' it said:

> You are my dear teacher. Comforter, sweetener, uplifter, my Gibraltar. When you read this my face will not be with you, but my heart will. I must loan you to our Beatrice for a while.[5]

Even while they were separated, Helen's influence was recognized. Charles' remarks, to one of his soloists, Ernest Naftzger, who had recently become engaged, was what a debt he owed to Helen and 'Tennessee'. Even with these bereavements, life and work continued but there was some joy that year in the marriage of her sister, Beatrice, although again, it would bring some sadness as Beatrice had lived with Helen since their mother's death. Early in 1912, Beatrice and her husband, Cornelis Boeke, set off to Lebanon as missionaries. The wedding, held in December 1911, was a happy family occasion with the added joy of the return to 'Tennessee' of Helen's sister, Daisy and her husband with their three children, who would stay at 'Tennessee' for eight weeks before staying in their own home in England for a while.

More journeys and campaigns

Once again, the travels and campaigns recommenced with the long journey to Australia and New Zealand. They set sail in February 1912 and did not return to England until June 1913. It was Charles' fifth visit to Australasia. On their journeys, at their stop off points, it was their practise to use these opportunities of preaching the gospel and visiting Christians in these various ports of call. The campaigns were a huge success. Helen was particularly conscious of the stresses and strains in the demands of the work on her husband and co-workers. There was the constant travelling, and meeting of people, old and new; supporting the co-workers; the organising of the choirs, the hymn books and hymn sheets; the constant publicity and the 'fame' that went with the work; and the huge success of large numbers attending the campaign meetings and professing conversion. Helen supported her husband through these trials and difficulties.

Helen's health issues

Helen, not only supported, but experienced some of these same difficulties for herself. She had become unwell during the Queensland missions with sharp pains from her appendix. In Melbourne they sought medical advice which confirmed she needed rest before an operation for appendicitis would be performed. With some anxiety, Charles went on with his campaigns, having to travel by ship to Western Australia—which at that time was unconnected by rail. Helen was left behind resting with the companionship of two ladies, Beatrice Atcherley and Clare Lelean. Charles left the Western Australian campaign ten days early and left the singing in the capable hands of Ernest Naftzger. On his return, he found his wife had benefitted from the month's rest. Then, three days later he took her to a private hospital where the operation was performed. He wrote her a note upon leaving her at the hospital and before he returned to the hotel which said:

> How I should love to have you in our beloved 'Tennessee', where we would not be away from you one moment. Our year-text must include this in one of the 'all things working together for good'. I know that this new set of people amongst whom you have gone will feel your strong, love-filled personality, and some may be saved as a result. I must not be too selfish, but lend you to other needy ones for a time.... He loves you, and I know His power is enough. I shall love the hymn 'Tis I, be not afraid!' since your sweet voice has hallowed it.[6]

The operation was a long and difficult one but was completely successful and, after a month's recuperation, Charles was able to take his wife to a mountain resort at Macedon, forty miles away from Melbourne. Before this short break, the Australian summer has been very hot and most of the co-workers and members of the party had a break, as the work had been tiring and demanding, especially with the effects of the heat. In spite of this, Charles continued to work on his hymn books as well as visiting the hospital. The new *Alexander's Male Choir* hymn book was published in Australia and Charles gathered male choir members to sing from it. This book brought blessings to many.

New Zealand mission

The next campaign was in New Zealand, but it was thought that the journey, not only to New Zealand but in the first area they were to visit, would be too arduous for Helen. So, it was decided, once again, that they would be separated for another couple of months. After her full recovery, it was felt that she would have regained enough strength to re-join them at Wellington. Helen endured this time of separation knowing that Charles was serving the Lord in reaching thousands with the gospel. After her rest and recuperation, Helen travelled to Sydney ready to depart for New Zealand. Just before her departure, a letter arrived from Charles which said:

> How glad I shall be to have you once more by my side to sympathize and consult with. Do not be afraid of the voyage alone. It will be calmer and warmer than ours was by way of Hobart. We are having splendid results here, and our party has been most harmonious. This Town Hall is much like the one at Sydney and almost as large. The days are packed with work, and I am thankful that I am keeping strong through it all ... Good-bye, sweet wife, until I see you at the Wellington wharf.[7]

Eventually, on April 9th, Helen disembarked safely from the ship to meet Charles, who rejoiced in their reunion and was overjoyed that she would be able to be with him in the closing meetings at Wellington, in New Zealand. Following this, they were able to have a few-days holiday and appreciate not only each other's company but the natural and cultural beauty of New Zealand. After this came the final series of meetings in Auckland.

Returning home

On May 10th, 1913 they set sail for home via Vancouver on board S.S. Niagara, after the long campaigns in Australia and New Zealand. As was usual for them, they formed good relationships with the fellow passengers and spent times witnessing to them. One fellow passenger, Mrs R. M. Fergusson, sometime later wrote to Helen and reminded her of the help which she had received from her. Mrs Fergusson had been particularly lonely while travelling on her own and she told of how she had appreciated their spirituality with the Bible readings and Gospel songs. Having arrived in Vancouver, Helen and Charles then set off across North America, but were able to go via the Rocky Mountains and have a break in Banff and appreciate the beauty of the area. Once again, a busy schedule followed with meetings at Moody Church, Chicago, and visits to reestablish old friendships, before they were able to renew some contact with Charles' family, who had now moved to Ohio. Finally, they set sail for England and arrived in Plymouth before making the final leg of the journey to their beloved home 'Tennessee'.

Home and work

On their return to Tennessee, more work was commenced on new hymn books, and in particular, *Alexander's Hymn Book No. 3*, with Robert Harkness and other assistants. These books were used for the various campaigns. Their home was again a hive of industry and hospitality, particularly over the summer. Further campaigns followed, this time in Scotland. At the end of the year some changes were made in the team of co-workers, with Ernest Naftzger being replaced by Albert Brown, as Naftzger was suffering with his health. Robert Harkness, who had been Charles' pianist for twelve years, felt that he needed to have a permanent home and income and he set up in business in London. It was a difficult task to replace Harkness, who was Charles' talented right-hand man. After many interviews and searches, Charles asked J. J. Virgo whether he knew of anyone and he suggested 'Barrie'—the nickname for Henry Barraclough. The only problem that Charles had with 'Barrie' was that he was a heavy smoker. It was during the interview that Charles challenged him to try to give it up, which he agreed to do and he never went back to smoking. Accordingly, this new team started the new year of 1914 with the continuing Scottish campaigns. Helen returned to 'Tennessee' during the Scottish campaign and wrote a message to her husband:

> It is exactly ten years by the date since thou and I wandered round the grounds at Uffculme, alone together for the first time, and passed where the snowdrops were pushing up through the snow. This afternoon, I took Kelly (a fine Irish setter) with me for a walk round the dear old garden, so altered in many places, but almost the same at that spot, except that the little pool and the summer-house, where we sat and talked so sedately, are now shut off by tall iron railings. The snowdrops are coming up in the grass, and I picked a few for 'auld lang syne.' As I stood there in the quiet, I thanked God for all that the ten years have brought us— precious joys and sacred sorrows, wealth of love and friendship, and above all, unique opportunities of winning souls to Christ, of circulating His Word, and of carrying joy and comfort and encouragement to thousands of hearts in many parts of the world through Gospel songs and hymns. Beloved, my heart is too full to utter my thanks to God for thee, and for all He has given me in and through thee, but He knows that I thank Him 'upon every remembrance' of thee. It was about four o'clock as I stood by the snowdrops, so I prayed specially for the men's and women's meetings in Edinburgh, and knew that my prayer was being heard for a great outpouring of the spirit of decision for Christ.[8]

Holiday break

Dr Chapman had experienced poor health during the Scottish campaign. Therefore, he was looking forward to returning home to America with his wife to have a break during the summer months and regain some strength. Helen and Charles, too, were to appreciate the break from the hectic schedules and were able to have a three-week holiday in Cornwall at Kynance Cove. They spent time enjoying their beautiful surroundings and being able to read the Scriptures together, and particularly studying the book of Daniel:

> Fellowship together with the precious Book of God strengthened and fitted them for the difficult service so soon to come through the troublous years of war, of which no shadow lay upon them in those peaceful June days.[9]

During the sunny days of June and July, the Alexanders spent three wonderful weeks amid the beauties of Cornwall at Kynance Cove—a lonely cleft between the cliffs, two miles over the moors from the Lizard Point. They stayed at Thomas's Hotel, an old mill adapted as a dwelling house, the only building in the Cove. Here, among the rocks and the boisterous waves and calling seagulls, they enjoyed another 'honeymoon'. Part of the mornings were spent in the quiet little room that had once been the mill-room, or sitting on the rocks outside, where they shared times of Bible-reading. They studied the book of Daniel together and were impressed more than ever that the time for the return of Christ must be drawing near.

During all this time, Charles and Helen were promoting the work of PTL at every opportunity but now, with some time set aside, they realized that they could not promote this work as much as they would like, with their busy schedules and travel. They decided to appoint dedicated staff and hired office accommodation in London. At the end of July, they spent some time at the Keswick Convention, followed by a short break in Scotland. Then, they returned home again for some rest and a time for preparations for the winter campaigns throughout England and Scotland.

'Tennessee' and the Alexander's home-life was an important part of their life in many respects. It was a haven for recuperation and recovery after the hectic travel and mission work but it was mostly a centre of busyness and hospitality with the overlap of both these aspects of life. Hospitality of the support staff for the missions and the preparations of new song materials and the production of new hymn books and publicity were intertwined with the extensive and often intensive hospitality for their numerous guests. In his book on the home-life of the Alexanders, J. Kennedy Maclean describes the significance of 'Tennessee' as the spiritual foundation of their married life and their aspirations, even though they were unable to have long stretches of time there together. The title of his book is, *When Home is Heaven* (the title was taken from a book of the same name, written by Alexander's co-worker Dr Chapman, but this time to use the title as an expression of the Alexander's home-life). Chapman originally wrote:

> When a home is builded after God's own plan; when the atmosphere is as He would have it, when the banner over it is love; when those who make up its completed circle are animated by the spirit of Him who always lived for others and never thought of Himself—then there is nothing on earth quite so much like heaven as a home.[10]

Maclean, a close friend of the Alexanders, knew them and their home-life first hand. Although it might be a slightly romanticized perspective, it reflects the importance and significance of the spiritual foundation of their marriage and their home-life and how they used their home for the good of others:

> Although it was never his [i.e., Charles'] privilege to spend many months in it [i.e., 'Tennessee'] at a time, it was ever the dearest spot on earth to him. Looking back over the years of his married life, and recalling the ceaseless activities which drew him constantly to America and to far-away parts of the world, … his thoughts turned homewards to the haven of rest and peace, where love was enthroned and where some of the sweetest and happiest days he had ever known were spent.[11]

A specially made fire-surround, made of wood, had the words, 'SECOND TIMOTHY TWO-FIFTEEN', carved onto the over-mantel, which took a central place in 'Tennessee'. The significance of this text on the fire-surround was so important that, even when 'Tennessee' was demolished after Helen's death to provide an old people's home on the site, this over-mantle was removed and repositioned in the new building. Helen had wished for her home to be used as an old people's home but, unfortunately, it was found to be unsuitable. Thus, 'Tennessee' had to be demolished with a new purpose-built accommodation provided instead but still retaining the name 'Tennessee'. Later, Richard Cadbury, Helen's half-brother, left a family copy of the biography, which Helen had written of Charles, to the new 'Tennessee' with the following inscription:

Charles Alexander and Helen Cadbury were married in 1904. The first Tennessee, built on this site was their home throughout their lives.

Richard Cadbury, a brother of Helen Cadbury Alexander Dixon, left this book to his son David. It has been given to the library of the new Tennessee (opened in 1974)[12] in the hope that the residents may like to know something of the builders of the original house.[13]

The outbreak of war

With the outbreak of the First World War, in 1914, a new venture came about. A new initiative from the dedicated staff of the Pocket Testament League resulted in Charles being invited to tour the British training camps at Salisbury Plain. This work resulted in thousands of New Testaments, gospels and hymn books being distributed, with many soldiers professing conversion. Dr Chapman returned to England and, in the September, he and Charles were taking meetings at the YMCA and at various training camps. Due to the war, Charles found that the normal outlets for their work were curtailed but there were many people asking them to undertake campaigns in America. Thinking that the war would be short lived and wanting to use their time and opportunities, it was decided that they would return to America. Before that, there was an urgent need to have someone to help Miss MacGill with the PTL work and Dr Fenn from Liverpool was appointed. He relocated to London, where he took up the post of becoming the Rector of a Reformed Episcopal Church as well.

Return to America

Accordingly on December 16th, Charles and Helen set sail for New York on the Lusitania with their more recent replacements of Albert

Brown and Henry Barraclough. Helen and Charles thought it would be a short time before they would return home, but Charles and Helen had to learn many lessons in trusting God. Normally their life was organized around the campaigns and work and they had envisaged returning to England, assuming that the British campaigns had just been postponed, but the war continued for the next two years. Plans were made and then altered; new ways were opened and others were closed; but many campaigns took place, and the PTL work increased. Both Charles and Helen had to learn to trust God in these unusual times. Even though things were organized at much shorter notice than they were used to, the travelling schedule of campaigns was gruelling on the health of both Charles and Dr Chapman. On their rest days, which were normally Saturdays, they would make the most of their day off with their wives and enjoy the times together.

Charles and Helen had booked a passage on the Lusitania for June 1915, only to find that it had been sunk by the Germans a month earlier than their booked journey. Therefore, it was deemed that they should remain in America, even though Helen longed to return home to England. During this time in America, just as in England, it was thought necessary to establish a permanent office with dedicated staff for the American PTL work. Again, as in England, once permanent staff were appointed there were more opportunities to distribute New Testaments to the training camps, as, by this time, America had joined the war. While Charles was regularly away visiting the camps, it was decided that Helen would be based in a house at Larchmont, about twenty miles outside New York.

Although she missed Charles, typically life for Helen was busy.

The Alexanders had come across a young Japanese girl called Haru Inoguchi at the conference in Northfield, USA. She had first met them in Tokyo, but she was now studying in America. Miss Inoguchi, while in America, had an operation and needed to recuperate and, sure enough, Helen offered her a home with her at Larchmont. She became a 'daughterly companion' and Miss Inoguchi referred to Charles and Helen as 'Oto-San' and 'Oka-San' (meaning 'Father' and 'Mother'). Another temporary daughter, this time an Australian, called Clara Lelean, needed a place to recover from an illness and, sure enough, another daughter was added to the household.

When Charles returned home, he always brought his young male workers—those who played and sang with him and helped in his camp visits. On occasions their niece, Helen—the daughter of Charles' brother, Homer—joined them for holidays. Not only this but Charles and Helen became the hosts at Revell Hall for the Northfield Conference speakers. During the summer conferences in 1915, while a group of them were out on a car journey through the beautiful woods, Mr. Barraclough composed a hymn which would become one of his most famous hymns:

> Turning to Alexander, he (i.e., Barraclough) said, 'I believe I have the words and music of a hymn on the subject of Doctor's sermon this morning.' Soon afterwards, the Alexander party were gathered round the piano, trying over 'Ivory Palaces', with its beautiful chorus:
>
> Out of the ivory palaces
> Into a world of woe.
> Only His great, eternal love
> Made my Saviour go.
>
> It is written in duet form, and as Mr. Brown and Mrs. Alexander tried

it over together, the tender strains of the music almost brought tears to the eyes of the little company. The new hymn was sung at the evening gathering of the conference, and was called for every night afterwards. Alexander realized that a message had been given in song which would bring joy and salvation to many a heart. In later conferences and evangelistic campaigns, it became one of the greatest favourites among the new songs.[14]

While they were in America, Helen's sister, Daisy with her husband and five children were in Victoria, British Columbia, Canada, when she was taken seriously ill. Helen and Charles travelled to assist. Fortunately, Daisy recovered, and Helen and Charles returned to America. During this time, Dr Chapman's health deteriorated and Charles found himself having to take on more work while Dr Chapman rested. Life was certainly busy.

Charles' accident

In February 1916, one Saturday morning in Pittsburgh, Helen and Charles were taken by taxi from the station to their hotel to have breakfast, when the taxi's 'steering-gear' broke and the taxi ploughed into an iron post on the footpath. Charles lunged forward into the glass screen and the glass severed an artery on his head. Dr Baldwin, a leading surgeon, providentially lived in this hotel and was able to save Charles' life. Helen nursed him during his time of recovery, although he suffered with severe septic trouble as a result. After two weeks, still with a dressing on his head, he was able to resume his journey to Washington Pa., not too far from Pittsburgh. This was another trial for them both but Helen and Charles again were able to trust God in this difficult and dangerous situation.

Death of Chapman

By September 1917, Henry Barraclough was conscripted to join the army and subsequently Leonard C. Voke (1899–1955) replaced him as Charles' pianist. Charles continued his work concentrating on the training camps. In November 1918, the Armistice was signed and the Alexanders could now consider returning home but, before they did, they were able to be part of a large Bible Conference in Carnegie Hall, New York in late November, joining with Dr Chapman, who was able to return to his preaching. In early December the two couples, Dr and Mrs Chapman with Charles and Helen, were able to spend a weekend together in a friend's home. They all appreciated this opportunity of renewed friendship and fellowship, with many hours of reminiscing. They assumed that their joint work, now that Dr Chapman had recovered, would soon restart, but this was not to be. On 23rd December 1918, Dr Chapman had to undergo surgery and on Christmas morning he died. For the past eleven years they had been like brothers and the two wives had been like sisters, and both Charles' and Helen's hearts were heavy with grief. This also left them in a predicament. It was a time for decision-making concerning their future, as they had now lost not only their friend but their co-worker in mission. For the time being, they made arrangements to return home to 'Tennessee' and be reunited with some of the family members.

A circuitous journey back home

Their travel back home was from the Atlantic coast to the Pacific Coast, to Los Angeles first, to conduct more campaigns—this time back with Charles' former evangelist, Dr Torrey! Helen was regularly called upon at these meetings by her husband to speak about the PTL. Helen and Charles spent much time renewing friendship with the Torreys. Later, Dr Torrey wrote to Helen saying:

> Everyone who knows you knows how you loved him, but very few knew all the romance of it, and the wondrous depth of your affection for him, as I do. I always regarded it as one of the most beautiful things I ever saw in all my life. I remember that I said, on the day when you were married, and Mrs. Torrey and I took the place of father and mother for Charlie, 'You think you love one another to-day, but you do not know what love means, as you will when years have passed by.' And I know you found it so. I was so glad to be with you in Redondo nearly two years ago, and to see how love had blossomed and ripened.[15]

They returned to the East Coast of America for more conferences, where they were enabled to enjoy renewed fellowship with George Stebbins and his wife—although, shortly after this, Mrs Stebbins suddenly died. Charles and Helen were ready to prepare for their journey home to 'Tennessee'. There must have been some sadness in their hearts as their close-knit community disbanded, with the two 'adopted' girls being left in America and many of the workers staying behind and finding new roles. Charles could not be without a pianist, so Leonard Voke returned to England with them. Charles liked the idea that Leonard would be reunited with his parents in England, as he was originally from England. In fact, Leonard later married Helen's niece, Irene and they adopted a daughter, Elizabeth Brenda. Eventually Charles and Helen arrived back at 'Tennessee' on July 18th, 1919, to a warm welcome.

Notes

1 'Honey'—from the very start of Charles' relationship with her, he often referred to her as 'honey'—an American expression of the time.

2 Fox, Simon, *Helen Cadbury and Charles M Alexander, A love that embraced the world*, p. 105.

3 Job 1:21

4 Alexander, Helen Cadbury and Maclean, J Kennedy, *Charles M. Alexander: A Romance of Song and Soul-winning*, p. 181.

5 Ibid., p. 174.

6 Ibid., p. 193.

7 Ibid., p. 196.

8 Ibid., pp. 200, 201.

9 Ibid., p. 202.

10 Maclean, John Kennedy, *'When Home Is Heaven'. A Brief Sketch of the Home-Life of Mr & Mrs Charles M. Alexander*, p. 3.

11 Ibid., p. 4.

12 Tennessee became sheltered housing but has now closed. However, it can still be identified on Google maps on Moor Lane, Birmingham.

13 With kind permission of the Cadbury family: C. Mary Penny, Helen's great niece.

14 Alexander, Helen Cadbury and Maclean, J. Kennedy, *Charles M. Alexander: A Romance of Song and Soul-winning*, p. 237.

15 Ibid., p. 242.

11 Helen: Life back home at 'Tennessee'

For the rest of the summer and autumn of 1919, Helen and Charles were able to entertain many of their family members and to have some of their nieces to stay with them. 'Tennessee' was full of a succession of guests and visitors in an attempt to catch up on all the lost time of separation while they had been in America. Seven of Helen's nieces, with various other family members who dropped by, spent a long weekend house party at 'Tennessee'. Each of the nieces kept a log of the weekend, which Helen and Charles created into a personalized scrapbook with accompanying photographs and materials. The nieces were:

- Dorothy (b. 1892), daughter of Barrow (Helen's eldest half-brother) and Geraldine Cadbury, who lived at 'Southfield', Edgbaston and who worked at Bournville.
- Geraldine (b. 1900) known as Cherry, also the daughter of Barrow and Geraldine.
- Eveline (Agnes) (b. 1903) and Beth (i.e., Elizabeth) (b. 1907), daughters of Richard (Helen's youngest half-brother) and Caroline Cadbury, from Worcester.
- Hannah, known as Joy (b. 1903), daughter of William (Helen's middle half-brother) and Emmeline Cadbury, from Wast Hills, south of Kings Norton, Birmingham.
- Elizabeth (Edith) known as Betty (b. 1902), and Christine

L-R Standing: Christine Butler, Beth Cadbury
Seated: Betty Butler, Joy Cadbury, Helen, Dorothy Cadbury, Geraldine Cadbury, Eveline Cadbury, Charles

Helen's nieces

(Winifred) (b. 1907), daughters of Edith (Helen's eldest sister) and Arnold Butler, from Stretton Croft, Barnt Green in Worcs.

The full text of the scrapbook is in Appendix 3, but a few comments are included here to reflect upon life at 'Tennessee'. Along with the nieces, came various other members of their families and some friends, visiting at different times over the long weekend and joining them for meals. This seems to have been a natural and normal way of life at 'Tennessee'. Charles and Helen seemed to have the weekend organized very well, obviously with their staff undertaking the various demands of the hospitality, Helen was sometimes absent, being busy behind the scenes but also ensuring that everything ran smoothly and orderly. Charles, in particular, seemed to have enjoyed the organizing of games, prizes, treats and activities. He enjoyed the use of his lantern slides in showing the nieces different parts of the world, as well as family scenes. Photography and memorabilia were important in the Alexanders' life and the very fact that each niece was given a scrapbook with accompanying photos is testament to that. In fact, the nieces were conscious of having their photographs taken especially by Mr Thomas, who was yet another of their long-term guests at 'Tennessee'. Mr Thomas was staying at 'Tennessee' to recover from his long months in hospital, after serving in France.

Music was central to life at 'Tennessee' and it was no different on this occasion, with Leonard Voke, Charles' accompanist and pianist, staying with them as well. There was much singing and learning of Leonard's songs, for many of which he had composed the music. Of course, they all sang the song, 'Tennessee' (see p. 164), for which Robert Harkness, Charles' previous accompanist, had composed the music in 1910. The songs sung that weekend were, 'We journey to a city', 'God will take care of you', 'I'll trust where I cannot see', 'Saved and Kept' and 'Whosoever will may come'.[1] With the musical skills of both Helen and Charles came

Helen and her nieces at 'Tennessee', 1919

their interest in poetry as well as Charles' ability to tell a story. Accordingly, the nieces were involved in reading poetry and composing their own poems and recounting and telling their own stories. Four of the nieces created a poem called, 'Song of the Nieces'.[2] Although there was much fun and laughter, there were serious times over the weekend and, of course, there was always the spiritual dimension to life at 'Tennessee'. The days always started and finished with prayer and Bible reading. Another example of the importance of spiritual things was that Charles gave the nieces the task of writing out what they each thought a Christian was and he followed this up with discussion. He also tackled a discussion with them on choosing a suitable husband! On Sunday, they went to the Friends' Meeting at Moseley Road. Each night, Helen tucked them into bed and gave them a good-night kiss, which reflected her love, warmth and care for them. The weekend made a great impression on these young relatives. The account in the scrapbook was personal, and yet it gives a great insight into life at 'Tennessee'.

The song, 'Tennessee'

At summertime, in sunny clime,
When we are faraway
On golden strands in southern lands,
Our thought will often stray.
To dear old Tennessee;
To dear old Tennessee.

Oh! dear old Tennessee of happy
memory,
Our thoughts go back to thee
Across the rolling sea,
And may there ever be
Peace and prosperity,
In dear old Tennessee,
Near Moor Green Lane,
Near Moor Green Lane.

'Tennessee' the song music sheet

We sing the praise of happy days
That live in memory,
And never yet can we forget
The hospitality
Of dear old Tennessee;
Of dear old Tennessee.

Around the world the flags unfurled
Wave proudly in the sun;
At Tennessee in amity
Three flags are rolled in one.
At dear old Tennessee;
At dear old Tennessee.

Whate'er betide, love shall abide,
Be dark the day or fair,
Though at His will come good or ill.
God's name is honoured there.
In dear old Tennessee;
In dear old Tennessee.

Oh, skies are blue and hearts are true,
And when we sail some day,
We leave behind strong cords that bind,
And never pass away
From dear old Tennessee;
From dear old Tennessee.[3]

This song, 'Tennessee', was written by William W, Rock, who had been Charles Alexander's secretary and the music was played by Charles' accompanist and pianist, Leonard C. Voke.

The staff at 'Tennessee' loved having the Alexanders back home and welcomed them back with open arms making an effort to have the home as welcoming as could be. The staff, some of whom Helen had known since her childhood, were dedicated to her. Both Charles and Helen were aware of the needs for the improvement of 'Tennessee' for the staff, after Helen's and Charles' long absence. Consequently, they agreed together in making arrangements for improvements, for the benefit of the maids and housekeeper. It was decided that an enlargement of the top storey could provide new bathroom facilities and that a change and rearrangement of the housekeeper's room could be made:

> ... while the room of the housekeeper, Eliza Shrimpton,—a member of the old household staff at Uffculme and for years the most faithful and devoted of helpers at 'Tennessee'—could be so altered as to yield extra space and give a window from which a fuller view could be obtained.[4]

Charles was keen to get involved in the arrangements. Unfortunately, the project took longer than expected to complete and more expensive than had been estimated. The housekeeper overheard Charles and Helen discussing these concerns and:

> ... coming quietly to Mrs Alexander, a little later, she confided in her that she was willing to hand over all her savings as a contribution, and to work in future without wages if need be. When I (J. Kennedy Maclean) heard this story from my daughter, I thought it was one of the finest tributes ever paid to Mr and Mrs Alexander; other and more

elaborate honours crowded upon them from time to time, but for genuineness and sincerity nothing could surpass this proffered gift of a deep and tender affection.[5]

J. Kennedy Maclean, the co-author of Charles' biography with Helen, had been Charles' secretary for many years and had travelled extensively with them. He really appreciated 'Tennessee', the home of the Alexanders, and went on to write a booklet about their home entitled, *When Home is Heaven*.

'Aliens' back home

Despite various members of the family being engaged in the war effort, no one in the family had lost their life, even though some had been in the army or navy and another in ambulance work. Although a joyous return home for the Alexanders, it was tinged with sadness seeing the after-effects of the war on the country, with its devastation and the dearth of men. It was odd to Helen that she was now treated as an alien, having to regularly report to the local police and having to secure an identity book. Obviously, Charles had to do the same, but for Helen it was strange that she was back in her own home yet treated as an alien. Mr and Mrs W. R. Moody came over from America to visit the Alexanders at 'Tennessee'. William Moody, the son of the famous D. L. Moody, was a close friend of the Alexanders. The Alexanders had covered the Moody's absence at the Northfield Conference, when the Moodys needed a break. Mrs Moody—Mary, known as May—was the daughter of Major Daniel Whittle, whom Charles knew. May had worked with Charles on editing the *Northfield Hymn book No. 3*, which was used at the conferences held at Northfield. Northfield is where Moody had built his home and had established his well-known summer conferences, on the site of the Northfield School. May was also a talented singer and musician; therefore, they had a lot in common with the Alexanders.

Beatrice, Helen's younger sister, who had lived with them for some time, was now living abroad in Holland with her husband and the four children she had by this time (she went on to have eight children in total). So, Helen visited this family in the Netherlands. Beatrice's life was complex[6] and Helen was very concerned about Beatrice's and her children's health and welfare. She sought to support them and, later, the ever-increasing family.

A Christmas visitor

Helen and Charles continued to work with the Pocket Testament League (PTL) in the UK and they spent many opportunities in promoting its work. The Christmas of 1919 was shared with an old college friend of Helen's, Miss Frances D. Shaw. She was a great-niece of Frances Ridley Havergal, the well-known English poet and hymn writer. She enjoyed a wonderful time and spoke affectionately of the warmth of welcome she received from both her hosts. Frances wrote:

The fireplace at 'Tennessee'

> My Christmas visit to 'Tennessee' is an unforgettable memory. Just previously I had been through a time of trouble and

anxiety, and I arrived on that bleak afternoon of December 23rd, 1919, a little tired in mind and body. Almost as soon as the hall door opened, a cheery voice said, 'Come in, come in, Miss Fan. When you once come in here you will leave all your troubles behind you.' A warm glow, physical and mental, enwrapped me at once. It was one of those wonderful flashes of intuition for which Mr. Alexander was noted— for he knew nothing at all, then, of my circumstances.[7]

Frances found that nothing was too much trouble for her hosts in making sure that all her needs were met. She shared in two large family gatherings on the Christmas Day. The evening party was full of fun and games but concluded with Charles' singing of, '*We journey to a city,*' and then with him praying. It was a wonderful uplifting experience for Frances to be part of the Alexanders' and their extended family's Christmas.

New Year visitors

A few days later, Mr and Mrs J. Kennedy Maclean, with their daughter and son, arrived at 'Tennessee' for the New Year celebration. They all stayed up to see in the New Year. Mr Maclean wrote:

> There were games for all, Mr and Mrs Alexander entering into the enjoyment of the occasion with a whole-hearted joyousness. A bran tub contained a variety of presents no one being omitted. The joy of my twelve-year-old boy, when a handsome camera bearing his name was uncovered, can easily be imagined. Soon after our arrival, Mr Alexander had talked cameras to his young namesake, and seeing the sparkle in the boy's eyes, determined to give him an up-to-date Kodak.[8]

(Charles had slipped out secretly to the town and had arranged for the purchase of a camera.)

As was their usual pattern, each day would be concluded with prayer and Bible reading and, if there were guests, Charles would often sing, tell stories and challenge the hearers to trust Christ. Helen and Charles were in complete agreement with spiritual aspirations for others to come to know Christ. In the biography of Charles, edited by Helen and by Mr J. Kennedy Maclean, it says of Helen:

> At one with him in all his enterprises and activities, Mrs Alexander shared with her husband the throne of their home. There, as in the larger world outside, they thought and acted together, and even in the simplest matters sought each other's advice and judgment. Thus, as the years passed, it became impossible to think of either of them in any relationship without also thinking of the other. More and more they blended into a perfect oneness, each depending upon and requiring the other; and within the sacred circle of their own home this closeness of heart and aim shone with a radiance that lifted the married state into an exalted sphere. With them, married life never degenerated into a commonplace or hum- drum relationship; it was the supreme expression of earthly felicity, never shadowed by a doubt or a misunderstanding. Lovers to the end, they walked together in shining garments down life's pathway, hand in hand, and heart in heart. Of all the endearing terms that fell from Mr Alexander's lips, nothing ever sounded so charmingly appropriate as the name 'Honey', as he often called his wife. It is frequently used among the warm-hearted people of the Southern States, but the word can be uttered without expression, and we may hear it a thousand times without

being impressed. To hear it, however, as he used to say it, suggested a tender affection that had no end.[9]

Return to America

In early 1920, Charles and Helen headed back to America for more campaigns and also to promote the American PTL work, which was growing. On Charles' departure, he wrote a note to the housekeeper of 'Tennessee':

> The days we have spent in our God-given home have gone by so swiftly that it seems almost a dream. My happiest days with Mrs Alexander have been spent while surrounded by all that makes our home. You have been part of it all, and we have prayed for you each day through all the years you have given your loving, splendid service—to think of home and happy times is to think of you, and the maids and the men who have made it possible. Thank you for the special care that you have taken this time of my precious wife. I am glad you all love to read and talk about the Bible and good things. Encourage this all you can. We shall be delighted to have any letters, any length, from any of you.[10]

Detroit was their first campaign city, with many thousands attending the meetings. On the last night, running in parallel to the main meeting, Helen ran a meeting about the PTL with about two hundred boys and girls, Helen questioned them about what they had done and found that over nine hundred had been signed up for the PTL during the campaign; such was the success of the work and the enthusiasm which the young people had to enlist others to read the Bible. They visited Moody Bible Institute and renewed friendships. Then, they moved on to Philadelphia for the next few months. On their last evening in America, they gathered together their friends and co-workers for an evening of fellowship and song before setting sail for England. Charles' sight was set on the mission work that he wanted to undertake in England.

Return to England

By the end of August 1920, they once again arrived home, Helen having learned to drive while over in America. Hence, they brought their new car over from America to England and were able to enjoy pleasurable drives around the countryside. They hoped they would be able to drive the car to either North Wales or Cornwall for a holiday before the main winter meetings. Even though Charles could drive a little, he had:

> ... great confidence and pride in his wife's driving and loved to call her his 'chauffeur'. Side by side in the car those sunny afternoons, they explored the roads and country places around Birmingham, seldom failing to fill the back seat with others who might share their enjoyment.[11]

Various meetings were arranged for the meantime and Charles did not mind how few people attended. He spoke to a Young People's Meeting at the Friends' Institute in Birmingham on Tuesday September 28th, where only about eighty were present but they all agreed to read the Bible daily. The following day found Charles in Southsea, near Portsmouth on PTL business. Later at Southsea station, Charles and Dr Fenn met a man who had a bookstall and Charles got into conversation and found out that he was a Christian. Charles challenged him to start a local PTL group and said that, if he did, the next time he was in Southsea he would present him with a

Testament. In fact, it was sometime later that Helen presented the Testament to him, having found out about Charles' promise.

The following afternoon, Charles arrived home feeling very weary but still his usual bright self. At home they had just one guest, a Miss Jenny van der Mersch. She was like a daughter to them; therefore, all of them shared a cosy supper together. In the night, Charles was awakened by the severe pain of a heart attack. After some medical assistance, he was relieved of the pain and fully recovered. With concerns for his health, the next few days' engagements were cancelled and Helen was able to take him on some countryside journeys by car.

Charles had promised to be the best man for J. J. Virgo (Jack), his musician friend, who was getting married on Tuesday 12th October 1920 in Birmingham. It was going to be a quiet wedding and, with a few more days of recovery for Charles, the doctor advised that Charles could go ahead with his plans as best man. Leonard Voke, Jack Virgo and Charles spent time together the day before the wedding. Voke had composed various new hymns and Charles particularly liked one of the hymns, '*Redeemed by the precious blood of Jesus*'. So, all four of them, including Helen, gathered and sang around the piano with Charles, who seemed to have regained his strength and enjoyed the company like the 'good old days'.

J. J. Virgo

John James Virgo (1865–1956), commonly known as Jack, was born in Glenelg, Adelaide in Australia. His father, Caleb Virgo—a carpenter by trade—and his mother, Mary, nee Swan, had eight children, with Jack being the eldest. He had a wonderful baritone voice. His father died so he had to work as a junior clerk. It was during his time that he providentially bumped into an old school mate, Oldham, who invited him to an evangelistic meeting. Jack's views of religion were intellectual and he was suspicious of the emotionalism of this kind of meeting, but he agreed to attend. Mrs Baeyertz, a converted Jew, was the evangelist and Jack was gripped by the experience of hearing her preach. He realized that his faith was dead, or as he called it 'static' but, after his conversion, it was 'dynamic'. He realized that, although he had been teaching Sunday School, it was not real for him and he was going through the motions, or as he called it 'parrot fashion'. Now his understanding was opened and he was teaching something that was living and real to him. He had an inner urge to serve God. He became the secretary of the Australasian Union of YMCA (the Young Men's Christian Association). He also started the Theatre Royal Sunday evening services for the youth, primarily to reach the unchurched young people of the city with the gospel. He visited other countries with his work and then became the travelling secretary for Australasia. It was during this role that he first met Charles Alexander, who would be Helen's future husband.

It was all through a mistake that Charles and Jack met. R. A. Torrey was organizing a mission in Australia and Jack oversaw the musical arrangements, as well as some of the secretarial work. Unknown to Jack, R. A. Torrey had arranged for Charles Alexander to travel from America to undertake the musical work. Charles arrived ahead of R. A. Torrey and went to visit Jack, who knew nothing of these arrangements. Finding out about this, Charles graciously offered to return home to America. Jack, seeing this forlorn figure, graciously withdrew from his post of musical director and handed it over to Charles Alexander. In reality they shared different parts of the role with Charles Alexander being the main soloist for Torrey. This incident was to prove the beginning of a long-lasting friendship. They met up again, this time on Charles' home ground of America, while Jack was travelling with the YMCA.

Jack later became the general secretary for the London branch of the YMCA. Once again, Jack met up with Charles Alexander in the Chapman-Alexander campaigns in London and renewed their friendship, this time with Charles' wife, Helen Cadbury. He visited the troops during the war and it was during this time that his wife died. He threw himself into the work to mask the feeling of loss. He was appointed the National Field Secretary, relinquishing his London role, and he now travelled to different parts of the world during the war. On one visit to France, he met his future second wife, Miss E. Dorothy Aston. She was providing practical help to the soldiers in the form of driving, looking after patients and their various needs. It was this wedding of Jack's where Charles was best man.

Notes

1 'We journey to a city' by Rev. H. Burton and music by Leonard C. Voke; 'God will take care of you' by C. D. Martin and music by W. S. Martin; 'I'll trust where I cannot see' written by Charles McCallon Alexander at the occasion of the nieces' houseparty with music written earlier by Leonard C. Voke but adapted for this creation; 'Saved and kept' and 'Whosever will may come' were both written and composed by Leonard C' Voke.

2 See Appendix 3: The nieces' scrapbook.

3 Ibid.

4 Maclean, John Kennedy, *'When Home Is Heaven'. A Brief Sketch of the Home-Life of Mr & Mrs Charles M. Alexander*, p. 20.

5 Ibid., pp. 20,21.

6 Joseph, Fiona, *Beatrice, The Cadbury Heiress who gave away her money*, (Birmingham: Foxwell Press, 2012).

7 Alexander, Helen Cadbury and Maclean, J Kennedy: *Charles M. Alexander: A Romance of Song and Soul-winning*, p. 247.

8 Ibid., p. 247.

9 Ibid., p. 248.

10 Ibid., p. 248–9.

11 *The Home-Going of Charles M Alexander*, pp. 7–8 in personal papers of the Cadbury family. By kind permission of C. Mary Penny, Helen's great niece.

12 Charles' death

After their evening of fellowship, friendship and singing, the wedding took place at noon the next day at Handsworth Church. Charles, as best man, was next to Jack Virgo and Helen sat next to Leonard C. Voke, a few seats away. When she looked towards her husband, this is what she saw:

> As Alexander stood with reverently bowed head by the side of his friend, such a heavenly radiance seemed to surround his tall, graceful figure, and the sweetness of his countenance was so strangely beautiful, she [i.e., Helen], sitting in one of the front pews, turned with a whisper to Mr. Voke, who sat next to her, asking whether he saw it. 'Yes,' he whispered back, 'isn't it wonderful!'[1]

Later, Helen and Charles returned to 'Tennessee'. Charles did not seem too tired and, after lunch, he felt well enough to stroll around the garden with Helen. He could not resist popping into the Den to look at the work on his hymn books but then was persuaded to take some rest. The home was empty of visitors, which was unusual, but this was to be short lived as Helen's sister, Beatrice Boeke, was due to be visiting them from Holland. Their housekeeper, Eliza Shrimpton, who had been with the Cadbury family since Helen's childhood, remembered seeing them being happy together during the day. Their normal practice of reading the Scriptures together and prayer concluded the day. Then, without warning, Charles suffered a fatal heart attack and, before any medical assistance could be summoned, he passed away from this earth into His Master's presence. Due to the Virgos immediate departure after

Charles' gravestone

their wedding to travel abroad to Sweden and other Scandinavian countries, they did not discover the death of their close friend, Charles Alexander, until much later.

> No tender yet sad farewell,
> From his quivering lips was heard;
> So softly he crossed the quiet stream
> That 'twas not by a ripple stirred.
> He was spared the pain of parting tears,
> He was spared all mortal strife;
> It was scarcely dying— he only passed
> In a moment to endless life.
>
> Weep not for the swift release
> From earthly pain and care;
> Nor grieve that he reached his home and rest
> Ere he knew that he was there.
> But think of his sweet surprise,

The sudden and strange delight He
felt when he met his Saviour's smile.
And walked with Him in white.[2]

What a shock for Helen! It was one of her fears that she would have to live without Charles. In her inimitable style, she faced this reality in prayerfulness and was able to find the Lord's grace was sufficient for her. She was able to trust her God and Saviour in all these kinds of difficulties. She remembered later the chorus they used to sing, which Charles had written and to which Leonard had composed the music:

I'll trust where I cannot see, Lord,
I'll trust where I cannot see.
No matter how dark the way may be,
I'll trust where I cannot see!

Helen would have to face her worst nightmare in living life without her beloved Charles by her side. Her precious 'Tennessee' would never be the same without him, even though it would continue to be her earthly home. She looked forward to being united with her Christ in the future and being reunited with her beloved Charles. It seems that Charles had the same nightmare of being left alone without his beloved and he had this in his mind when he penned the following in his notebook:

One of us, dear— but one—
Will sit by a bed, with a marvellous face
And clasp a hand
Growing cold, as it feels for the spirit-land.
Darling, which one?
One of us, dear— but one—

By an open grave will drop a tear
And homeward go.
The anguish of an unshared grief to know;
Darling, which one?[3]

Helen had placed her own New Testament, which she had carried with her for years under the pledge of the PTL, into the hands of Charles' body. He had promoted the work of the PTL but, more importantly, he had trusted in the Scriptures and the God of the Scriptures. He had always signed his name Charles M. Alexander, followed by the Bible reference, 2 Timothy 2:15, which reads, 'Study to show thyself approved unto God, a workman that needeth not to be ashamed, rightly dividing the word of truth.' This signature and Bible reference were inscribed on his coffin. On 16th October 1920, Charles' funeral took place and his body was laid in the family grave at Lodge Hill Cemetery, Birmingham where a section was allocated for the burial of Quakers. The cemetery was not open later in the afternoon; thus, the funeral took place at 12.30pm, which meant many could not attend. Despite this, over three hundred people gathered around the graveside. The grave, which also has the inscription for their baby who only survived a few hours, was next to the grave of Helen's father and mother. (Although later Edith Butler, Helen's elder sister, along with her husband were buried in between Helen's and her parents' graves.)

The coffin bearers were the Rev. W. Talbot Hindley of London; J. Kennedy Maclean (Editor of 'The Life of Faith'); two nephews, Paul S. Cadbury, and William Cadbury Butler; Leonard C. Voke (Mr Alexander's pianist), and F. S. Turney (his assistant in the preparation of hymn-books). Behind the coffin followed Helen with her sister,

Beatrice, from Holland, and various other Cadbury family members. Others followed: Miss E. W. MacGill and Dr J. Louis Fenn represented the PTL (Field Secretary); Miss A. Laurie-Walker and Miss Frances Maclean; Mr J. Barnett Gow; Rev. Edward; then, Rev. Walter Young and Mr Clarke of Southampton, followed by Friends and representatives from the Friends' Meeting and Institute. The American Consul was present and Mr Gracey, who also represented the American government. Some members of the Young People's Service from the Midlands Institute sang.

The service at the graveside was simple with Dr Fenn leading it, beginning with the hymn 'The Sands of Time are Sinking'. Helen's brother-in-law, Arnold Butler, read John 11:21–26; 1 Corinthians 15:51–58; 1 Thessalonians 4:13–18; and Revelation 22:17, 20–21. Helen's half-brother, Richard, prayed; then followed the hymn, *'Jesus, Lover of my soul'*. After this, Helen's uncle, George Cadbury, spoke and Beatrice, Helen's sister, prayed. The closing message was given by Dr Fenn of the PTL. He spoke on the threefold passion of Charles Alexander's life: for Christ, for the Word of God and for souls. A plea for anyone who did not know Christ as their Saviour was made. Finally, the service closed with Lowry's hymn:

'What can wash away my stain? Nothing but the blood of Jesus'

What can wash away my sin?
Nothing but the blood of Jesus.
What can make me whole again?
Nothing but the blood of Jesus.

O precious is the flow
that makes me white as snow;

no other fount I know;
nothing but the blood of Jesus.

For my pardon this I see:
nothing but the blood of Jesus.
For my cleansing this my plea:
nothing but the blood of Jesus. (Refrain)

Nothing can for sin atone:
nothing but the blood of Jesus.
Naught of good that I have done:
nothing but the blood of Jesus. (Refrain)

This is all my hope and peace:
nothing but the blood of Jesus.
This is all my righteousness:
nothing but the blood of Jesus.
(Robert Lowry, 1826–1899)

Despite her sorrow, Helen was able to pray aloud and thanked God for 'the sixteen years of heaven upon earth'. Then, 'The Glory Song', which had been the one that was so closely associated with Charles, was sung as the crowds dispersed. One of the verses was particularly appropriate:

When by the gift of his infinite grace,
I am accorded in heaven a place,
Just to be there and look on his face,
Will through the ages be glory for me.

This verse was also inscribed on his gravestone.

These are the words of 'The Glory Song' by Robert Harkness which

are included here, again, to easily compare it with Helen's hymn
that follows this:

> When all my labours and trials are o'er,
> And I am safe on that beautiful shore,
> Just to be near the dear Lord I adore
> Will through the ages be glory for me.
>
> *O that will be glory for me,*
> *(O that will be glory for me,)*
> *Glory for me, (Glory for me,)*
> *glory for me (glory for me!)*
> *When by His grace I shall look on His face.*
> *That will be glory, be glory for me!*
>
> When, by the gift of His infinite grace
> I am accorded in heaven a place,
> Just to be there and to look on His face
> Will through the ages be glory for me.
>
> Friends will be there I have loved long ago;
> Joy like a river around me will flow;
> Yet just a smile from my Saviour, I know,
> Will through the ages be glory for me.[4]

Helen wrote the hymn, 'After the shadows have passed away',
with the title 'The Glory of Heaven'[5] reflecting similar sentiments
as the 'Glory Song':

> After the shadows have passed away,
> From my life forever,
> When I have entered the land of day,

Just beyond the river;
Then with what joy my heart will thrill,
Eager His face to see;
Glory and peace my soul will fill,
Glory enough for me.

That will be glory enough for me,
Glory, glory,
Seeing the Saviour who made me free,
Glory, glory;
Close by His precious side to stay
All through eternity,
That will be glory bright as day,
Glory enough for me.

Resting at last on that golden shore,
Free from sin and sadness,
Weakness of earth will be mine no more,
Serving Him with gladness;
If I may gain His blessed smile,
Rich my reward will be,
That will be glory all the while,
Glory enough for me. (Refrain)

With my beloved ones gone before,
What a glorious meeting;
Safe in His presence to part no more,
Heaven's joy completing;
Even while here on earth I wait,
Strengthened my soul will be,

As I behold that glory great,
Glory enough for me.

This hymn, which Helen wrote, is poignant in reflecting a time in her life of sadness and shadows but her rejoicing in the passing of these times and looking forward to meeting her Saviour in heaven. Now knowing that her beloved Charles had gone before her into God's presence, she knew she would be reunited with him in the presence of their precious Saviour. This Saviour had made them free from the penalty of death and now she rejoiced in the hope of union with Christ and her loved ones. But the main theme coming through is that of glory, which fits with the famous '*Glory song*' that was so associated with Charles and his work. In Helen's hymn, the refrain emphasizes this theme of glory and reiterates the glory that will be in heaven in the presence of the Saviour.

During and after the funeral, many were challenged to seek the Saviour and to read the Scriptures. Some of Charles' friends took the opportunity to speak to the coach and taxi drivers. Three days after the funeral, Helen and her sister, Beatrice, went to take roses to the grave at the request of Charles' mother and family and went to thank the head-gardener for all the arrangements. Even then, Helen was able to challenge the head-gardener and his wife about their need of a Saviour.

Many messages flooded in for Helen following the death of Charles, expressing their appreciation of him and his work. Many wanted to celebrate his life; therefore, a thanksgiving service was arranged, although some of his friends and relatives were unable to attend. On the evening of Wednesday, October 27th, a thanksgiving for Charles was arranged at the Birmingham Central Hall, led by Rev

T. E. Titmus—the only surviving secretary of the great Bingley Hall Mission of 1904. Helen was on the platform with many of her family members and friends in support of her. It was still hard to be able to get many of Charles' friends and co-workers to be present, as they were far flung in different parts of the world.

Leonard C. Voke, his pianist, was able to play and one of Charles' soloists, Mr William Andrew, was able to sing, as well as two young women singers. The women sung a hymn which had been requested by Charles' mother: 'The land where the roses never fade'. Leonard C. Voke sang his own new song, 'Redeemed by the precious blood of Jesus', which, although so new to Charles, had already become a favourite. Twelve hundred people attended and various speakers. Rev. J. Stuart Holden, an old friend of Charles, who took his place as president of the PTL for Great Britain early in the war, spoke. Rev. W. Talbot Hindley, one of a group of Cambridge students who in 1905 had become a Christian through Charles' mission, spoke. The messages called sinners to repent and turn to Christ. This was a fitting conclusion to the life of Charles: for thankfulness to God; the proclamation of Christ and his gospel; and the plea for sinners to turn to Christ.

A special private memorial service was arranged in New York by Mrs McAnlis, the secretary of the PTL in New York. About three hundred friends attended; Dr John McNeill, a close friend who had met Charles in 1893 at the Moody Bible Institute, conducted the service. Many others participated and spoke personally of the effect of Charles upon their lives.

As the news spread around the world, more messages arrived at 'Tennessee' with expressions of sorrow and shock but with appreciation for the live and work of Charles. Another thanksgiving service was organized in the YMCA's Tottenham Court Road premises on November 23rd. Here, Jack Virgo was able to chair the service and sang, 'The land where the roses never fade', and shared memories of Charles. Other memorial services were held in different parts of the world and throughout the UK. The Moody Bible Institute and Northfield each held memorial services. The news of his death seemed to give impetus to the work of PTL. More effort was made to reach the 'street car' men in Philadelphia (street cars were trams or trolley buses); to set up more prison work promoting the reading of the Bible; and starting work in the industrial plants and various other institutions. Dr R. A. Torrey became the president and Mrs J. Wilbur Chapman, and Helen became vice-presidents of the United States of America PTL, with the aim of increasing its promotion in churches and other religious organizations.

Life without Charles

A huge void was now left, having lost her husband and the work and travels that they used to undertake together, with the many campaigns all over the world. Her life was to take a different direction, albeit with some of the same work, in that she threw herself even more into the PTL work, of which she was not only the founder but the International President. The PTL work increased all over the globe and, by 1936, it had over five million members with many of its own missionaries. There are many testimonies which can be given because of the distribution of the Bible and the work of the PTL.

One outstanding testimony is by Mitsuo Fuchida, who was the

lead Japanese pilot at the bombing of Pearl Harbour. He was converted by reading his Bible and, later, he met with the head of the Pocket Testament League in Japan, who encouraged him to read the Bible, pray and witness. He realized that he needed to witness of this new life in Christ and he spoke in the open air. He shared how he had been a man of war but now he was a man of peace because he had peace with Christ. Fuchida went on to be an evangelist.[6]

Helen had been used to such a busy life and she was still full of energy; therefore, as well as working for the PTL, she busied herself with entertaining her family and, particularly, her young nieces and nephews. She had always been used to a home full of visitors, so she continued to entertain guests and missionaries, as well as providing facilities for gatherings in the old Tea-Sheds in her grounds. Later, she had a meeting hall built, which was more functional for these occasions and opportunities. Helen's visitors' book ran to numerous volumes! She decided that she would also collaborate with Maclean, Charles' friend and previous personal secretary, and write the biography of her husband Charles, with many photographs added to the publication. This work must have been a mammoth task, although they had already collected and collated all their memorabilia and photographs to use as a resource. (The biography was thought to be published in 1920, the year of Charles' death, although it was not originally dated. I think it would take longer than a few months for the biography to be written, but because there is a dated poem inscription included by Barrow Cadbury, which is dated October 13, 1920, it seems to have been assumed that this was the date of publication.)

The following is a transcript of a letter which Helen enclosed in a copy of Charles' biography that she sent to the Pocket Testament League members:

'Tennessee'

Moss Green Lane

Birmingham

Dear Friends of the Pocket Testament League

I hope that the life-story of my dear husband may bring to you not only a share in his sunshine, but a strengthening of faith, and a fresh impulse to witness boldly for Christ. Shall we not carry forward with enthusiasm the Bible Revival for which he worked and prayed so earnestly 'holding fast the faithful Word' and 'holding forth the Word of Life'?

Your friend in Christ,

Helen C. Alexander

[signed with her own personal handwritten signature that you can see on the front cover]

Rom. 1. 16[7]

The following poem was written as a tribute to Charles by Helen's half- brother, Barrow; it was included in the biography. He seems to have captured the essence of Charles Alexander's character and the Biblical text which so summarized his goal in life—to be a workman for His Saviour. At the same time, there are references to some other aspects of his life: his singing; his love shown in deed and word; his 'sowing' of the seed and Word; his leading others to Christ; his happy face. There is also a challenge that others will now have to carry on the work of sharing the gospel. Finally, there is the reunion in Heaven. This poem was included as a tribute in some copies of Charles' biography:

Charles M Alexander

Approved of God, a workman not ashamed,
The Word of Truth, ever by thee proclaimed,
In joyous song, in loving deed and word,
Sharing the joy and presence of thy Lord.
Sower and reaper over all the earth,
How great thy work, how precious is its worth,
How many greet thee on the heavenly strand
Whom thou didst lead to Jesus by thy hand.
And thou, dear workman, who didst serve so well
Thy Lord and Master, and His love didst tell,
Art still amongst us, though we fail to see
Thy happy face, we still are near to thee.
Bearing to Heaven, thy sheaves of golden grain,
From fields of labour, weariness and pain,
At that fair haven and celestial shore,
Thou'rt safely landed to return no more.
Of seed thou sowest, others are reapers now,
And we must still on earth the good seed sow,
That we may all in Heaven with thee rejoice,
Hearing the 'well done' in our Saviour's voice.

> October 13, 1920
> Barrow Cadbury[8]

Notes

1 Alexander, Helen Cadbury and Maclean, J Kennedy, *Charles M. Alexander: A Romance of Song and Soul-winning*, p. 258.
2 Ibid., pp. 258, 259.
3 Ibid., p. 259.

4 The words and music of 'The Glory Song' were written by Charles H. Gabriel (1856–1932).

5 https://hymnary.org/text/after_the_shadows_have_passed_away

6 There are many books and accounts of Fuchida's story. *For that One Day: The memoirs of Mitsuo Fuchida, the Commander of the attack on Pearl Harbour*, is a translation of his memoirs into English, by Douglas T. Shinsato and Tadanori Urabe, (Riverside, CT: Experience, Inc., 2011).

7 Found in a copy of Alexander's biography.

8 In the Library of the University of California, Los Angeles' digitized copy of *Charles M. Alexander: A Romance of Song and Soul-winning* by Helen Cadbury Alexander and J Kennedy Maclean, 1920. Sourced on archive.org.

13 Marriage a second time around

Helen certainly never thought of remarriage. But she had an unexpected meeting with A. C. Dixon[1] (Amzi Clarence)— known as Clarence, or sometimes just A. C.—a widower whose wife had died while they were visiting China. He had been a longstanding friend of her late husband, Charles, but he had also developed a friendship with them both after Charles' marriage to Helen. Clarence and Charles originally met at the Chicago World Fair in 1893, when Moody was organizing evangelistic missions in the city. He invited A. C. Dixon to preach at some of the meetings which were scattered over the city and it was on one of these occasions that A. C. Dixon was allotted Charles Alexander as his song leader. Alexander at this time was a student at the Bible Institute. Alexander and Dixon struck up a friendship which was made firmer as they were both 'Southerners'.

A. C. Dixon

A. C. Dixon (1854–1925) was born in Shelby, North Carolina to Christian parents, Thomas and Amanda Dixon; his father was a Baptist preacher. Clarence followed in his father's footsteps. When his father went preaching for two weeks at an evangelistic mission, he took along his young son, Clarence, who was probably about twelve years old, and challenged him about his soul. During one of the sermons, Clarence was struck by his sin and need of a Saviour and claimed that he was purely trusting Christ as his Saviour. Later, he was part of a group of a hundred people being baptized. Clarence studied hard and, because of his academic abilities, he graduated with the highest honours of his class. He thought he would become a lawyer, but he felt the call to be a preacher.

At the young age of twenty, he became the preacher at Bear March and Mount Olive Churches for a year, having deferred his theological training which he had started at the Baptist Theological Seminary, South Carolina. After a year at these churches, when he was due to return to the seminary, he was offered the pastorate at Chapel Hill, North Carolina, which he accepted. He met Susan Mary Faison, whom he referred to as Miss Mollie, and later he married her. He went on to be a pastor at various churches but he also wanted to reach out to the masses with the gospel. He took every opportunity he could, including open air work and hiring large venues, to preach the gospel and to especially reach the poor. In 1893, he was involved in Moody's outreach at the World Fair, where he met Charles Alexander. Little did he know what the outcome of this new relationship would be. Dixon met up with Torrey and Alexander after their return to America from their UK campaigns to see what he could learn from them. He was the pastor at Immanuel Baptist Church, Baltimore; Hanson Place Baptist Church, Brooklyn New York; Ruggles Street Church, Boston; Moody Church, Chicago; Metropolitan (Spurgeon's) Tabernacle, London, England and finally the University Baptist Church, Baltimore. During these pastorates he led evangelistic missions not only in America but other parts of the world, and he also taught and preached at conferences and Bible colleges.

At one of the Northfield Conferences, he met, Ada Habershon, an

English Bible student and speaker at the ladies' conference. It was this Ada Habershon who would later become one of Charles Alexander's hymnwriters back in England and become a close family friend. At one of the meetings in London, when Clarence was visiting there and attending the Torrey-Alexander missions, he met for the first time Alexander's English wife, Helen. His comment about her was that 'in the young English woman he (i.e., Charles) had married, God has given him a wife whose love for Christ and his work is an inspiration'.[2] This was the start of a friendship between the Alexanders and the Dixons. When Clarence was the minister at the Metropolitan Tabernacle, London, when the war broke out, he was in the middle of some evangelistic meetings, so he invited Chapman and Charles Alexander to take over a few days of his mission. They were able to do this due to the cancellation of Chapman-Alexander missions because of the news of the war. Clarence Dixon was gracious in not wanting to have the limelight to himself and he wished to use the talents and gifts of Chapman and Alexander.

While Clarence Dixon was the minister at the Metropolitan Tabernacle during the war, he declared his allegiance to pacifism. During the first winter of the war, he found himself alone—his wife was unable to be with him as their daughter's prolonged illness had detained her. Although he was lonely without her, he was glad that she was not part of the war-torn country. His work was time consuming, but he appreciated the offers of hospitality of his friends. On one visit to the Alexanders, Charles recommended him to have a Steinway Grand for the Metropolitan Tabernacle. On another visit to the Alexanders, he wrote to his wife:

Last Friday I went to Birmingham ... and spent a night with Charlie Alexander in his English home, which he has named 'Tennessee', Charlie and his wife simply revel in the joy of their love for Christ and His work. Some of our time was spent in telling stories, talking of old times in the United States, and Charlie and his singers gave many beautiful Gospel songs. They insisted that I should come there any time I wanted to, whether they were at home or not, and I am sure they meant it. Many times you were spoken of, and the wish expressed that you could be with us. As I was about to leave, one of Alexander's soloists sang 'God will take care of you,' and Charlie called on Mrs Alexander to lead in prayer. She did pray for you and the children so sweetly that I am afraid I wept. I could but say to them as I told them goodbye, 'you have given me a bit of heaven' and surely it was so. They sail for America in December. I hope you may see them.[3]

Dixon continued his work and outreach not only in London but also in Ireland, where he had commitments. Later, he sailed to America, for a three-week reunion with his family, knowing that the 'Lusitania' had been sunk and that the journey was dangerous, but the vessel he sailed in was clearly marked in large letters, 'American Line' (as at this time the USA was not part of the war). He and his wife, Mollie, had the joy of seeing their daughter, Clara, married to Frank Howard Richardson, before they returned to England. Little did they know that, when they sailed from New York on 11th September, it would be four years before they would be able to return to America as the USA would join the war. (The reverse of the Alexanders who were left in America, unable to return to England.)

The war conditions in London were difficult for the couple and Mrs Dixon's health suffered as she worked alongside her husband, with the pressures of the scarcity of food and the awful smog of London. He decided that his wife should stay in the Surrey countryside to improve her health and gain some strength, but he continued his work in London, and not only in London—he often travelled great distances to preach but always returning to London in time to preach there as well. He would find time to visit his wife and take along his manuscripts to discuss with her, although travel became more difficult with the air raids. During this time, he received offers of meetings back in America but, along with his wife, they concluded that the time was not opportune. Yet, they would have loved to return to America, having received the news of their daughter, Clara, giving birth to their first grandchild.

During the summer they were able to have a holiday and chose to travel to Scotland. While in Oban they travelled to the island of Iona, only to find that they should have completed forms declaring themselves aliens and were now unable to return to Oban—thus left in limbo! They sent out pleas and eventually permits were granted them to return to the mainland.

Extra outreach work, called the 'Trench Campaign', ensued in London. The secretary of the PTL, Miss E. W. MacGill, originally from America, who was a member of the Metropolitan Tabernacle, became one of the workers in this. One joy during this time was that their son, Faison, had to make an unexpected visit to London; they had not seen him for over four years as he had been working in Venezuela. Later, it was decided that Mrs Dixon should move to Droitwich, and then Somerset, to avoid the dangers of the effect of the war on London. The Metropolitan Tabernacle's basement was open every day as a place of protection. Dixon continued to travel all over to take meetings, as well as at the Tabernacle, but his health suffered and, in early 1918, he had an acute seizure of neuritis. This time it was he who was sent to Surrey for recuperation and Mrs Dixon returned home, saying that she was never going to be away from him again. Eventually the war ended on November 11th, 1918.

With the end of the war, A.C. Dixon and his wife felt for the first time that they could think about the future and make decisions. They had received many requests, especially about returning to America. On New Year's Eve, they received the news from Charles Alexander concerning the death of Chapman. Later, having digested this news of this great gospel preacher, Dixon thought about asking Charles to join him in gospel work for a year. Charles and Helen were still in America and had commitments; therefore, they declined the offer. Dixon took this as a confirmation, alongside other events and thoughts, that he should leave the Metropolitan Tabernacle and set off on a new venture.

With various preaching engagements in America, on his way to Los Angeles he settled at his new work for a few months of the year at the Los Angeles Bible Institute and the Church of the Open Door. He had opportunities to work on other missions throughout the year. He was also a fervent supporter of the Pocket Testament League. More offers of speaking at conferences and missions came in and he thought about joining forces with Charles Alexander in this work, only to receive the news that Charles had unexpectantly died. Dixon continued his conference work and campaigns and was happy in this role but, unexpectedly, a different course opened to him—one which he thought he had relinquished.

The University Baptist Church's trustees in Baltimore were so concerned about Bible truths, considering the attacks of modernism, that they begged Dixon to consider serving as a short-term pastor for the beginning of this new church. Consequently, A. C. Dixon and Mrs Dixon found themselves not only back in pastoral work but back in Baltimore. The 'first few months' of the short-term work lasted for two years! Then, he was offered a permanent position, which he accepted on the basis that he could spend some of his time on evangelistic campaigns and fulfil some of the work to which he had already committed himself. In particular, he wanted to work out in China, which had been planned before taking up the short-term pastorate. He had agreed that he would support the work, out in China, at conferences to promote the sufficiency and inerrancy of Scripture in the fight against modernism. Thus, in the summer of 1922, Mr and Mrs Dixon set sail for China. He spoke at various ports of call before arriving in Shanghai and speaking there, before travelling to other parts of China.

On one of the boat journeys in China, at about midnight, Mrs Dixon felt unwell and, on disembarking, she was taken to a missionary doctor who examined her and thought there was no cause for concern. That day was extremely hot and Mrs Dixon fell into a deep sleep. It was felt that Mr Dixon should continue his arrangements for the evening meeting. Mrs Dixon became very ill with a high temperature and it was decided to move her to the hospital, where she seemed to improve—so much so that she encouraged him to return to his preaching. He was able to fulfil some of his commitments and returned to find her improved, but then she deteriorated and developed meningitis. The doctors confirmed that she would not recover. He decided that he would preach and then return straight way afterwards to his wife, knowing that she would want him to preach. It was at the end of the sermon that he received the news that his wife had died. The last address of the conference turned into a memorial and thanksgiving meeting for the life of Mrs Dixon. She was buried in a grave in the green hills of Kuling. A Chinese choir sang, 'There is a happy land, far, far away', a Chinese worker prayed, and A. C. Dixon read 1 Thessalonians 4.

The following day, A. C. Dixon wrote:

> A great empty world! My heart is buried in China, but for the sake of Christ I must keep on with my work. The Lord Jesus Christ is the only one who can take the place of everybody and everything that He may see fit to take out of our lives.[4]

How similar this experience was for both Helen with the loss of Charles and Clarence at the loss of Mollie. Both couples had travelled the world with the aim of making Christ known; both Helen and Clarence felt that no-one could replace their beloved partners in marriage and in Christ.

A. C. Dixon remained in Kuling with the cooler weather, before completing some more of his conference speaking and then returning home. Like his friend, Charles Alexander, he too would use the opportunities on board ship and at various ports of call to preach the gospel. He, then, returned home to Baltimore to settle into life without his wife. Many thought of A. C. Dixon as unusual because he had the gifts of not only being a teacher but a pastor and an evangelist.

Helen and Clarence Dixon's marriage

While working abroad in 1923, Clarence visited England once

again—this time alone—and it was while he was in London that he once again met Helen Cadbury Alexander. Clarence, unexpectedly, found that he now considered remarriage for the first time as he developed a love for her. He thought that she would be a wonderful companion and co-worker alongside him. Neither had Helen contemplated remarriage and, at first, rejected its possibility. Yet, a bond of friendship through their similar situations of having lost their beloved marriage partners developed into something deeper, which was bound together with their spiritual lives and aspirations. Clarence wrote to one of his daughters:

> It is like a dream … that I am to have my dreary loneliness banished … No one can ever take Mother's place with us, any more than I can take Charlie Alexander's place with her, but I know that God has given her for a blessing. The fact that my children are pleased about our marriage gives me great pleasure.[5]

This marital union was helped by the fact that Helen was an American citizen and had not only been married to an American previously but had lived and travelled in America. They both had many common friendships in America and Britain. In writing to his sister-in-law of Helen, Clarence wrote:

> Though born in England, Mrs Alexander, is an American citizen and a hundred per cent American in spirit and sympathy … She is of Quaker family with wide Christian sympathies, and will be a great help to me in the life-work that remains.[6]

Consequently, on 25th January 1924, Helen, aged forty-seven, and Clarence, aged sixty-nine, had a quiet wedding in London, at St Jude's Free Church of England, Balham. This was followed by a few days honeymoon in Cornwall, one of Helen's favourite places. While on their honeymoon, he was recognized by some of the locals and, therefore, it was arranged that he would preach on the Sunday in Mullion at a gathering of Nonconformists. They had become familiar with his message through *The Christian Herald* and other religious magazines.

After their return to Helen's beloved 'Tennessee' home, which would continue to be their English home and, like her previous married life, would become a place of spiritual and physical refreshment for her new husband, preparations were made for them to cross the Atlantic. It was a very familiar journey for Helen but now, with her new husband. A. C. Dixon was once again back preaching at the

The wedding of Helen Cadbury Alexander to Clarence (A. C.) Dixon

University Church in Baltimore where Helen was introduced to the congregation. Clarence, now with Helen beside him, commenced afresh his work of preaching, evangelizing and teaching.

A. C. Dixon seemed reinvigorated in his work with his new wife and companion by his side. He believed his life's motto: 'God's work in God's way with God's power to God's glory.' He had a pastor's heart, and it was his practice to carry in his pocket a notebook containing the names and details of the church members. He would use these lists to pray for each one, especially making use of his time when travelling. It was through this notebook that Helen became acquainted with the names of the many people she was introduced to in the early days of her arrival in Baltimore. A. C. Dixon resumed his preaching and teaching but the idea and opportunities of large evangelistic campaigns seemed to be dwindling in the eyes of many, which saddened him.

As well as working in Baltimore, he also travelled during the week with his 'wife and comrade in the service of the gospel'. From March to July, he spoke at conferences in New York and Atlanta, Georgia, then Ohio, as well as his old church, Moody Church, Chicago. This seemed a familiar way of life for Helen; one that she had been used to with Charles but now with Clarence. A short break was spent with A. C. Dixon's children and his grandchildren in North Carolina. Here they were able to appreciate the beauty of the Black Mountains and have some time of refreshment before they returned to England, where a full programme for the rest of the summer lay before them.

Part of the summer of 1924 was spent back in England at their 'Tennessee' home, where Helen resumed her role as hostess with many guests, including many travelling from America. Her sister, Daisy, and her husband had returned for the summer to 'Tennessee' to be with their children. Three of these children were like adopted children to 'Aunt Helen' and lived at 'Tennessee' while their parents were in China. Clarence slotted into the role of host quite easily. He had preaching engagements in Scotland and various Pocket Testament League Meetings. A. C. Dixon spent three of the August Sundays preaching at Charlotte Chapel, Edinburgh, as well as preaching at Carruber's Mission and the Railway Mission. The short intervals between these preaching engagements were spent in the Scottish Highlands with Helen who was accompanied with her niece, Helen Alexander. They enjoyed the beauty of the Highlands, the lochs and the heather. As they drove back home to 'Tennessee', they passed through the Lake District and viewed its natural beauty. On their return they conducted more PTL meetings. In England much of their time was taken up with the Pocket Testament League work and the Bible League but Clarence was able to study and write letters and booklets as well, making use of the garden and the 'garden shed'.

Then, Helen and Clarence set off for a mission in Sweden. Once again, Helen was on her world travels supporting the gospel work of her husband; this time instead of her beloved 'Charlie' it was her new husband, Clarence. Both men had the same desire as her for the salvation of sinners. They attended the 10th anniversary of the Dutch Pocket Testament League in the Netherlands. On their return, they broke their journey at Paris to see Mary Dixon, Clarence's daughter, and her work there; Mary had opened a student hostel for Christians. Clarence preached to both English and French audiences—the latter by means of an interpreter—and he also spoke at the Bible Institute.

After the summer they returned to Baltimore, where they continued together in their work there. It was during this time that Clarence received a letter to ask him whether he would become Dean of the Los Angeles Bible Institute. Since Dr Torrey had left, there had been divisions in theological matters and it was felt that A. C. Dixon would be the man to teach and lead the college. With the support of his church, he said he would visit for a few weeks to help, especially as he had been there previously and knew the situation. Reflecting on his decision to not take the deanship he, later, wrote:

It was perfectly clear to me that I could not accept the call to the deanship of the Los Angeles Bible Institute, though I thought it worthwhile to cross the Continent to give what help I could. My wife and I returned to Baltimore with renewed conviction that we should give ourselves as far as possible to the important work here.[7]

Clarence's illnesses

While there, and on his return journey, he suffered the first severe attacks of pain at the base of his spine and decided to consult a doctor as soon as possible. Arthritic rheumatism was the possible diagnosis but, at the same time, his health was made worse by problems with his teeth—which were extracted. His mouth became infected and he had a series of operations. During his convalescence, he meditated on the various theological movements that were prevalent in the American situation of the time, with the conflicts and controversies between Modernism and Fundamentalism. In the end, he resigned his membership of the Baptist Bible Union of America, preferring to work through the church rather than para-church organization. The issues that came from this conflict would continue to echo through the early part of the 20th century.

On March 1st, after only a short absence from the pulpit of the University Baptist Church, Baltimore, Clarence resumed his preaching. Despite the recent theological turmoil of his resignation from the Baptist Bible Union of America and dealing with the issues of Modernism and Fundamentalism, he preached on, 'And ye know that all things work together for good to them that love God, to them that are called according to His purpose'. It was amazing that, just a short time after major dental surgery, his articulation was clear. Life was busy with many scheduled meetings and, on top of that, a major new auditorium was being planned. Much as they would have loved to travel back to France to see Mary Dixon, Clarence's daughter, and the French Bible Institute's work, they had so many commitments planned for the summer back in England that it was impossible for them to squeeze in a visit. Clarence also wanted to take some time apart in preparation for a heavy workload over the winter.

Various treatments were tried to relieve him of his pain and, despite this, he carried on with his pastorate work, but reluctantly had to cancel some engagements which were further afield in different parts of America. He planned to preach on 'Christ in the Bible' over the next couple of years and to cover this subject systematically through each book of the Bible. Again, in spite of his pain and discomfort, he was able to stand and preach and appeared to have increased strength in his preaching. But, behind the scenes, he was deteriorating in his health and was suffering extreme pain that baffled the doctors. He was advised to reduce his workload, especially during the week, and take rest. He dictated a letter to a friend, Mr Manning:

> I have been confined to my room for a while … No cure had yet come, though the teeth, which were said to be the cause of my trouble, were removed six weeks ago. I am trying to keep up my regular work at the prayer meetings and of preaching on Sunday, but shall have to beg my friends excuse for a while from all outside engagements.[8]

He continued his study while bedridden, particularly as he wanted to prepare four sermons that he hoped he would preach on Sunday afternoons, tackling the differences between Fundamentalism and

Modernism. He wanted to emphasize the Bible as the foundation of truth and faith and he was able to see the fruits of his labours in being able to preach these sermons.

Clarence's death

In an attempt to relieve his pain, he was put in a plaster cast but this was unsuccessful and, after three weeks of discomfort, it was removed. Helen cared for him during these difficult and harrowing times. He managed to preach the Easter sermon but then all his future engagements were cancelled to help his recovery. Good speakers were arranged to cover his absence. His four grandchildren and their parents, Clara and Frank Richardson, took an opportunity to visit him on their way to their mountain home, at that time not knowing that they would not see him again. Helen continued to care for him but eventually it was recognized that he needed constant nursing care and on May 4th he was taken by ambulance to Union Memorial Hospital. His only living son, Faison (named Abner Faison), had just returned from South America, arriving in New York. Therefore, he and his wife made their way to Baltimore to see him. Mary, his daughter in France, was cabled and she too arrived to be near her father. They were able to be with their father for the last week of his life. At the same time, another family sadness occurred when Clarence's youngest brother, while on a lecture tour, contracted pneumonia and died at his home in Brooklyn. Clarence was not informed of this loss.

While in hospital, he gave out New Testaments to the nursing and medical staff, like both Helen and Charles had done, and encouraged them to read the Scriptures. All three of them had the same concern that the seed of the Scriptures would be sown in people's hearts and that, in the Scriptures, the wonderful gospel of the Lord Jesus Christ would be declared because in them are the words of life. Clarence had once said that, given the choice of a quick death or a slow lingering death, he would have preferred the former. Yet he had been given a period of six painful months before his final departure from this life of pain and suffering. On Sunday June 14th, 1925, he died.

A funeral service was held two days later at the University Baptist Church, Baltimore. Dr W. L. Pettingill, the Dean of the Philadelphia Bible School of the Bible, who had been covering the preaching on the Sunday along with two others of Clarence's friends, took the funeral service. A solo was sung of 'God shall wipe away all tears'. Dr W. L. Pettingill, who knew of A. C. Dixon's dislike of eulogies, chose to read extracts from Clarence's own book, *The Bright Side of Death*. He was buried in Druid Ridge outside Baltimore with his motto text engraved on his headstone: 'Worthy is the Lamb that was slain to receive power and riches and wisdom and strength and honour and glory and blessing' (Revelation 5:12). Later that same day, a private service was held in their Homewood Apartment where hymns were sung and memories were shared. Helen was once again a widow but having been a co-worker alongside both her husbands in their service together for the gospel and their Saviour: Charles for his song and soul winning and Clarence for his preaching and soul winning.

Notes

1 A. C. Dixon was called Amzi Clarence Dixon. Although he was more personally known as Clarence, he was mostly referred to as A. C. Dixon or even A. C. and, on other occasions, Dr Dixon and even Amzi Dixon — mostly

I have chosen to refer to him as Clarence or A. C. Dixon.

2 Dixon, Helen (Cadbury) Alexander, *A.C. Dixon: A Romance of Preaching*, (New York & London: G. P. Putman's Sons, 1931), p. 158.

3 Ibid., pp. 215–216.

4 Ibid., p. 262.

5 Ibid., p. 296.

6 Ibid., p. 296.

7 Ibid., p. 308.

8 Ibid., p. 312.

14 Helen's later life

This was not the end of Helen's service for her Saviour, as she was to live another forty-three years as a widow. Being an American citizen (in the US one could not hold dual citizenship until 1967; in fact, it was not until 12 May 1936 that Helen became a British citizen by re-admission[1]), she continued to live, at this stage, in America but frequently sailed back and forth to England until 1938—presumably the war curtailing her visits. Helen continued to live in Homewood Apartments in Baltimore where she had resided with Clarence during their short-lived marriage. It was natural for her to return home regularly for visits to 'Tennessee', as she had made regular and frequent Atlantic journeys throughout her life. Helen's and Clarence's plans had been to return to 'Tennessee' for the summer, as had been Helen's normal preference, so after Clarence's funeral she returned home at the end of July

Helen with her two sisters, Daisy (middle) and Beatrice (right), at Helen's 90th birthday

1925. From that year up until 1938, at the age of sixty-one, she sailed across the Atlantic at least twenty times. It is clear on some of the passenger lists (the latest record in 1931 which showed her residence) that she was still residing at Homewood Apartments and on the passenger lists 'Tennessee' is referred to as her temporary accommodation! Although she was an American citizen until 1936, she acted as if she had dual nationality. Some of these American visits lasted about four months but occasionally longer. She was able to maintain contact with the Dixon family,[2] especially his daughter Clara, her husband Frank and the four grandchildren. After 1936, when she was now a British citizen, she named Frank Richardson, her son-in-law, (Clarence's daughter's Clara's husband) as the person she was visiting in the USA. Her last recorded visit by ship to America was at the age of sixty-one. She obviously regarded Clara and Frank as close family members. At the age of sixty-one, on the passenger list she is recorded as being 5 feet and 5 inches with clear complexion, grey hair and hazel eyes—her well-recognized, sparkling hazel eyes![3]

As with her first husband's biography, she now undertook the writing of a biography of Clarence, her second husband, entitled, *A C Dixon: A Romance of Preaching.* The book is dedicated to Clarence's family: 'to the children and grandchildren who are his dear gift to me', reflecting her fond affection for them.[4] While still living in Baltimore, she researched material for her second husband's early family history up to his death with all the family's background, just as she had done with her father's and her first husband's biographies. She once again used her writing abilities to produce this book which reflects not only the character of Clarence but his many achievements and works, along with his many trials and difficulties. A collection of his materials, letters and sermons were kept at the Southern Baptist Historical Library and Archives, which Helen trawled through in her research. She also attended a reception given in her honour at the Hanson Place Chapel, in 1928, where Clarence had been the pastor—this was prior to the celebration of its 75th anniversary. *The Brooklyn Daily Eagle, New York,* reported on this reception and also added about her research:

> The Brooklyn Daily Eagle, New York, Saturday February 11th, 1928
>
> Reception Honors Widow of Pastor
>
> Mrs H C A Dixon is Guest of Hanson Place Church
>
> A reception in honor of Mrs Helen Cadbury Alexander Dixon, widow of the Rev. Dr Amzi Clarence Dixon, who served as pastor of the Hanson Place Baptist Church between 1890 and 1901, was held last night in the prayer meeting room adjoining the church. The reception was one of a series of functions, reminiscences of earlier days in the historic church which have been arranged by the pastor, the Rev Dr Mark Wayne Williams to mark the 75th anniversary of the church next year.
>
> Mrs Dixon who lives in Baltimore was born in England, the daughter of Mr Cadbury, the British chocolate magnate and philanthropist. She married the minister, who was one of the outstanding pulpit preachers during his 10-year ministry here, less than two years before his death in 1925. In addition to his work in Brooklyn, Dr Dixon served as pastor of various churches in Boston, Chicago and London.
>
> Mrs Dixon is engaging in writing a biography of her husband and requested members of the congregation to help her in the task by furnishing anecdotes of the minister. Several members of the church

gave interesting sidelights on the character of the former pastor of the Hanson Place Baptist Church.

In order to carry out the reminiscent character of the service last night Dr Williams led the congregation singing some old hymns which were compiled by some members of the church.[5]

Not only did Helen research and write her husband's biography, but she also undertook some research to produce a Historic Sketch of the University Baptist Church, Baltimore, MD.[6] from 1917–1926. It started with the inception of the church and Helen's now-deceased husband being its first pastor in 1921—initially short-term but, in 1922, becoming fulltime until his death, in spite of losing his first wife during this time and, of course, marrying Helen. After his death, the church continued its building plans as well as seeking a new pastor, although Rev James S. Kirtley became the acting pastor for a time before Rev. Russell Bradley Jones, from Kentucky became the permanent pastor in 1927. The proceeds for the sale of the booklet were donated to the building fund.

While in America, after the loss of Clarence, Helen 'read a paper' called 'Intercession for Revival'[7] which she gave at the Quarterly Meeting of the Women's Missionary Union of Southern Baptists, in Baltimore on January 5, 1927. This organization had been developed by Clarence and his first wife Mollie. The paper was produced as a booklet by Moody Press as one of their Evangel series of booklets. Obviously, Helen, with her experience of 'worldwide revival', especially with the tours she made with her first husband but also with her short but more limited time of revival with Clarence, would be a well informed and experienced speaker to tackle the subject. Her extensive biblical knowledge along with her prophetical views, are evident in the booklet as well as her ardent zeal for the proclamation of the gospel. At the beginning of the paper, she stated, 'This address is issued with the desire of helping the prayer-service of all who can unite in this request—"Thy kingdom come. Thy will be done on earth as it is in heaven."'[8] She tackled false ecumenism and universalism; she dealt with Old and New Testament covenants and promises; and the prophecies relating to the end times. She concluded with the challenge that true Christians should be witnesses of Christ and, in praying for revival, we pray for increased unity of true believers and that these ones are to love, work and pray without ceasing.

Helen viewed 'Tennessee' in England as her home, even though she did not become a British citizen again until 1936. Until this time she lived several months at a time in America and then returned to England, crossing the Atlantic many times. Helen continued in the beloved work of the Pocket Testament League, and especially supported the American work when there. She hosted various Christian events at 'Tennessee'. The first international conference for the PTL was held at 'Tennessee' in 1928 where it was affirmed that the work of the PTL was worldwide uniting all the countries in their promotion of reading the Scriptures and carrying the Testament with them daily. Helen had always thought that 'If we could only get people to read the Book for themselves it will surely lead them to Christ'.[9]

Helen, on becoming a British citizen again, had another thirty or so years ahead of her. It has been difficult to discover much about these years as most of the insight into Helen has come through her writing of her father's and her two husbands' biographies as well as the lives of her husbands, who were in the public arena while she was alongside them. Glimpses of her later life have been discovered but, unfortunately, many of the personal artefacts have been lost and very few people who had been close to her are alive at the time of this writing. However, a few snippets have been discovered and give a picture of some of her later life.

Helen and the Adult Institute work

During the early days of Richard Cadbury's Adult Education work, it had been felt that the wives of the men were neglected in their provision. A Monday afternoon women's meeting had been started by Emma, Helen's mother, who became the President. Emma took much of the responsibility for its running along with a band of helpers. The Sunday morning Adult School times were difficult for some of the women to attend, so a daytime opportunity was sought which also offered a creche for young children. Originally, when the women factory workers married, they were unable to continue their employment at the factory, as it was felt that it would put too much pressure on the family life. Even the male factory workers thought that there should be some more provision for their wives. With the provision of the new Stirchley Adult Institute building, there was more than enough space for the women's meeting to be held there.

Mary Penny, a Cadbury descendant, remembered that the meetings were advertised in the women's cloakrooms at the factory and that any women at the factory were given permission to attend during the day. It was a religious service with hymn singing and Bible reading with a talk but there was opportunity for help and care for the women. In 1908, there was a membership of just over 250 with an average attendance of about 140. With no National Health Service, there was a sick club where funds provided help for the sick. There was a benevolent fund which assisted in the provision of gifts and help, including distributing clothing. Many charitable visits were made by the members. A choir led the singing and Helen donated the Alexander hymn books for this purpose. An annual outing took place, which was the highlight of the year for many who had little experience of travel away from home. Many attendees of the meeting became members of the Pocket Testament League, regularly singing the hymn, 'Take it wherever you go'. Although Helen did attend the meetings in her earlier days when she was at home and would occasionally speak, later in life she attended regularly and when she was ninety years old, she became its President! This was after the death of Emmeline Cadbury, who had been its President.

Helen enjoyed taking on the responsibility of the organization of the Christmas tea, which had been a tradition in memory of Helen's mother, Emma, whose birthday was on Christmas Day. On the records there were 88 names, with an average attendance at the meetings of 65, so who knows how many came to the Christmas tea! With dwindling numbers at the meeting, it continued until 1984, seeing many changes along the way. It was the hope that the link with the Pocket Testament League would in some way continue the original aim of the women's meeting of sharing the gospel and the Scriptures.

The Almshouses

The Almshouses, often known as the Quadrangle, because of the design around a lawn in the shape of a quadrangle, had been a particular vision of Richard Cadbury. Helen continued to take an interest in its residents, particularly identifying with the older and often widowed occupants. She was a frequent visitor to the residents and often entertained them in her home on special occasions. Her work with the Stirchley Women's Meeting involved charitable work in caring for the elderly residents.

Helen and the family

Helen loved children and continued to be involved with the growing number of children in the family. The children of Daisy, Helen's younger sister, had virtually been adopted by Helen in the days of Daisy and her husband working out in China. The children had lived

Bournville Almshouses Christmas Party, 1948

at 'Tennessee' and later, when Daisy and Neville returned to England, she continued this fond relationship. Daisy's first child was called Marguerite Helen. In all, Daisy had six children. Emma Denham, who had been the children's 'nurse' at Uffculme, when Emma, Helen's mother, died, had her employment transferred to 'Tennessee'. Eliza Shrimpton, who was the parlour maid, had also transferred from Uffculme to 'Tennessee'; these faithful and long-serving employees were two of the mainstays in helping with the running of the home and for the care of the children when Helen was away from home. Helen maintained contact with lots of friends and, in her death, she made provision for her employees and their relatives as well as family members, including her stepchildren, even though she had only been married to Clarence for less than two years. Personal recollections of her, viewed her as disciplined and determined, yet with a wonderful warmth and love. One of her relatives remembered her as giving 'smacking kisses' and that she had beautiful, smiling eyes. She adored children and loved the family but was always considerate of others outside the family, especially those in need.

Helen's continuing hospitality

Hospitality continued to be a focal point of her life at 'Tennessee'. Many 'parties' or gatherings of the family took place, especially with the beloved nieces and nephews, increasing to the great nieces and great nephews as Helen grew older. Helen often attended the Christmas Day celebrations with her half-brother, William, and his family, and the children viewed her as their splendid Aunt Helen. They remember singing Helen's favourite carol, around the Christmas tree, 'Hark the Herald, angels sing'. Some of the Cadbury family traditions continued or were adapted. Richard Cadbury's family Easter tradition was to hide the hot cross buns in the garden for the children to discover, while another branch of the family hid the hot cross buns on the roses in their garden, to be associated with the thorns of the cross. Sometimes 'Tennessee' became a short-term home for relatives who required accommodation. Regular Christian meetings and house parties were hosted at 'Tennessee'. She attended conferences and Christian meetings, and some remember meeting her at the Keswick Convention.[10] Amy Wang Sit (1925–2008), the daughter of missionaries, Dr Lelan and Ada Wang, who at the age of fourteen emigrated to America on a full music scholarship, stayed at 'Tennessee'.

> I stayed three months at the house of a dear lady who was the founder of the Pocket Testament League, Helen Cadbury Alexander Dixon. Her father founded the Cadbury Chocolate Company. She taught me how to speak English. She never called me 'Amy' alone. It was always 'Amy darling' or 'Amy love'. She spiced her addressing of names with love. To this day (almost 40 years later) I cherish the memory.[11]

Personal reminiscences

Leith Samuel wrote in his autobiography about an incident where he met Helen Alexander Dixon at 'Tennessee' in the late 1930s:

> While I was studying for the General Ordination Examination of the Church of England at the Queen's College, [the theological training college, Birmingham] the BUECU held its annual Houseparty at 'Tennessee' the hospitable Moseley home of Mrs Helen Alexander Dixon, nee Cadbury of chocolate fame…. A most delightful lady to talk to, she had founded the Pocket Testament League…. Her zeal for the spread of the gospel was unabated to her dying day!
>
> It was my privilege as one of the speakers to stay in the house and to sit next to our hostess at several of the meals. I will never forget her first husband's life motto: 'Only one day at a time to live, only one person to please!' And that person was not Helen! But when Charles pleased his Saviour, he could not help pleasing his wife, because all she wanted for him was God's best at all times and in every way—as all the best Christian wives do for their husbands![12]

Later, Leith Samuel wrote[13] about his involvement with the Hyde Park Witness team which he led for ten years. His interest had been originally sparked by the contact he had had with the '*One by One*' band, which had merged with the Pocket Testament League. From the Pocket Testament League work started by Helen, links were made with other evangelistic works in preaching the gospel.

Someone who belonged to King Edward High School in Edgbaston, in the 1940s, who was a member of the Moseley Crusaders, remembered attending one of the Crusader meetings in the grounds of 'Tennessee'. The seniors would go into the side room where the walls were filled with the photos of the Torrey-Alexander Missions. He remembered that many Christian meetings were held on the summer Saturday afternoons at 'Tennessee' and that the PTL's hymn, '*Carry your Bible*', was often sung. Later in life, when he was organizing a missionary meeting to be held at 'Tennessee', he had to meet with Helen to make arrangements; he found her a 'formidable lady'.

Another Christian, Stanley Jebb, in his blog, in an article on, 'Acknowledging Indebtedness', refers to Helen and 'Tennessee' and the influence and effect she had on him and others:

> It is so easy to forget those who have taught us and shaped our lives. When I think about it, I am so grateful to God for those who have influenced me for good and taught me the things of God...
>
> The various ministers, lay preachers, evangelists, conference speakers all played their part, in emphasising the importance of the inspired Word of God. I remember the conventions and conferences held in the very large garden of Mrs Alexander Dixon's in Moor Green

Lane, Birmingham. Mrs Alexander Dixon (nee Helen Cadbury) was founder of the Pocket Testament League.[14]

Continuing relationships abroad

'Tennessee' and Helen were intertwined with each other. It was the centre of her work of hospitality and service. It continued to be the case for the rest of her life. Her close and extended family members were frequent visitors and many friends and visitors continued to find a warm welcome from her. She maintained relationships with her stepchildren, her step-grandchildren in both America and France, as well as keeping in touch with more distant overseas relatives, such as her great niece and great nephew in New Zealand. She maintained contact with family members over many years, keeping in touch with Charles' nieces—the daughters of his brother, Homer—Helen Louise and Olive Bertha, known as 'Oddie'. Obviously, it would take much of her time in keeping in contact with all these relatives in different parts of the world as well as in England. She continued to be a busy letter correspondent, having done this for most of her life. She continued writing to her stepchildren and step grandchildren and others from around the world but especially to her second home of America. In the following letter she shows that she had maintained a relationship with George Stebbins, who had worked closely in writing gospel songs and accompanying Charles Alexander in his missions and refers to himself as Uncle George.

> From: George Stebbins
> 83 High Street, Catskills, N. Y.
> Dear Helen,
>   What a flood of memories are awakened by your Christmas

greetings! They came back one after another and leave a blessing. It is so kind of you to keep me in mind when you have so many friends to think of and claim your time and thank you for it with a full heart. I have been thinking of Amzi's later years as spending your winters on this side of the sea which makes your greetings from the other side just at this time a surprise. And yet I should be very sure you would be with your home people in this time of their danger.[15]

... I am thankful to say that I am keeping and feeling well all the time and that my sister is now in good health though as yet unable to walk owing to her fall in the spring causing a break in one of her limbs. We are hoping, however, that ere long she will have strength back. I am thankful to say also that our Bertha continues well for the most part and is ever our greatest comfort and joy. And God is with us in His gracious love and care.

Bertha joins me in love to you, dear Helen, and thanking you again for thinking of me.

Yours gratefully and affectionate, Uncle George[16]

Helen and music

Helen continued her interest in music and she was able to sing until she was ninety. Most days she also played her violin, being a member of an orchestra and a quartet. One of her great nieces remembered that Helen sang in the City of Birmingham Choir; although crippled by arthritis she would 'appear at the top of the raised seating, shining in a white dress and billowing white hair, waving her two sticks, before making a perilous descent to her place'.[17] As she aged, her beautiful voice deteriorated and it was suggested that maybe a retirement age of ninety should be brought in by the choir! She was a member not only of the City of Birmingham Choir but also the

Choral Union and the Bach Choir. She loved the hymnals that Charles had published and regularly sang from them.

Helen and hymn writing

Helen's love of music started at an early age, and it was a common bond, particularly with her first husband, but this love continued into her old age. Helen had written a few of her own hymns[18] and she also arranged hymns for other writers. She added two verses[19] to an earlier hymn of Jessie Pounds ('Anywhere with Jesus'), as well as adding to and altering other hymns and adding extra stanzas to a few hymns that others wrote.[20] The continued publications of the Alexander hymns and hymn books were overseen by her and she ensured that the copyright of hymns was up to date. Why Helen chose to write additional stanzas to some of these hymns we can only surmise but, in some cases, there seems to be an added urgency for the sinner to come to Christ which would fit in with her concerns for soul winning. The hymns which were associated with the PTL and its promotion would remain dear to Helen's heart because of the ongoing connection with the PTL throughout her life; hymns such as 'Carry your Bible'; 'Win Someone'; and 'Hide God's Word in your heart'. Each of these hymns carried important sentiments by which Helen tried to live out her life.

Youth organizations

During the 1920s, the PTL had formed its own choir—later it was renamed the Ambassador's Choir—but this discontinued after some time. However, when two young Americans came to England preaching, in 1946, from *Youth For Christ International*, they revitalized many of the Christians to engage afresh in evangelistic and, especially, in young people's work. The names of these two men were Billy Graham and Cliff Barrows. During these campaigns, the PTL choir was reformed and used for the Birmingham meetings. Then, because of the success of the work, a new *Birmingham Youth For Christ* association was established using the already existing work of the Young Life Campaign, introduced by the brothers Frederick and Arthur Wood, and the Crusader Union group. This was another offshoot of the work of the PTL, which Helen had started.

Helen's continuing friendship with Robert Harkness

Helen was a good friend in maintaining relationships with many people over the years. An example of this is Robert Harkness, who had been Alexander's pianist for twelve years. Robert Harkness had been chosen by Charles Alexander to be his pianist during one of the Australian campaigns—Robert being a native Australian. It was through Charles' exhortation for Robert to consider eternal things, that Robert, who had Christian parents, considered his need of a Saviour and was converted. He travelled with Charles all over the world. He was with Charles during the time of the Birmingham mission where he met Helen Cadbury for the first time. Upon Charles' and Helen's marriage, Robert Harkness and others became the 'boys' working with Charles and often staying at 'Tennessee' or nearby 'Kentucky'. Robert later married Adele Ruth Langsford, a fellow Australian. She was a singer and together, after Robert had separated from his partnership with Charles, set about in travelling, holding concerts and working with music.

Robert continued to be an avid author and musical composer of

*Inscription on the side of Charles' grave for Robert Harkness, reads:
'Also Robert Harkness of Australia, died May 8, 1961 in London, aged 81
years. Composer and pianist to C.M.A. for twelve years'*

hymns. He wrote over 2,000 hymns and the music for the well-known hymn, 'He will hold me fast'. He composed songs, especially for the Pocket Testament League. He and his wife eventually settled in the USA where she died. After her death, he continued to travel and tour. On one of these missions, he was involved in a car accident and suffered a serious injury to his jaw. It developed into cancer and Helen arranged for him to be treated in London, at her expense— unfortunately, he died after the operation. Helen, being a kind and close long-term friend, arranged for his remains to be buried at her husband's and child's grave back in Birmingham. Robert had been such a part of Helen's and Charles' early life and had been one of the 'Tennessee' boys, working on hymns, music and hymn books, as well as lantern slides.

Helen and Leonard C. Voke

Another long-term friendship which she had, was with Leonard Carl Voke. Although English, he travelled with Charles for many years in the USA as his pianist, after Barraclough, the pianist, was drafted into the army. Eventually, Voke returned to England and met Helen's niece, Irene—the daughter of Jessie Cadbury Clarke, Helen's half-sister. Later, he married her. He was another one of the 'Tennessee' boys and he too wrote songs for the Pocket Testament League. He died and was buried in Lowestoft, England.

Helen and refugees

Helen also helped in bringing quite a few Jews out of Germany and Austria before the start of the Second World War—again typical of her nature and concerns for others. She became personally responsible for the safe transit of many Jewish families escaping Nazism, via Basel, whom she housed in 'Tennessee'. She had converted part of her home into a self-contained flat so that these families could feel that they had their own home, before they were found permanent accommodation. Two Austrian refugees, Ernst and his wife, Olga Rote (Roth), were living and helping at the house and gardens at 'Tennessee' in 1939; surprisingly they were given some money in her will! The Quakers were very involved in the refugee programme for Jews fleeing from Nazism. In 1914, 'Uffculme', itself—the old family home—was used to provide shelter for refugees from Belgium. In 1939, there were various other visitors, including Helen Louise Alexander, her niece, who was staying at 'Tennessee' from Detroit, USA, recovering from an illness, as well as two Chinese evangelists staying with Helen. During the Second World War, 'Tennessee' was also used for victims of the bombings in Birmingham.

Active until the end

Later in life, Helen developed arthritis but remained energetic despite this infirmity, although it did prevent her from driving—which was one of her loves over many years since importing a car from America. She was an extremely determined woman, and nothing would stand in her way when she was determined. Despite the extreme arthritic pain, she went the extra mile in her hospitality. She would often stand to shake hands with four to five hundred visitors at her garden meetings or escorting international visitors around the Cadbury factory and Bournville estate, or even taking them sight-seeing. Alongside the religious meetings she attended at the Stirchley Institute, were opportunities for the provision of social welfare. During her later years, she had a stroke, but she even recovered from that! In 1962, at the age of 85, when the Eric Hutching's evangelistic campaigns were taking place in Birmingham, Helen was knocking on doors inviting people to attend. In 1967, Helen was able to celebrate her 90th birthday with family members, some of them coming from overseas. The celebration was held at the Birmingham Botanical Gardens where over seventy guests joined Helen for her birthday. The autumn before she died, she took time to present a Pocket Testament to the

Helen and Daisy at Helen's 90th

Helen's 90th birthday

Names of guests in photo for Helen's 90th

Mayor of Birmingham. A friend and PTL worker, Ivy M. Lawrence said that Helen had remained remarkably active up until the year before her death and had attended the local prayer meeting when she could, had supported local causes and had maintained the Saturday meetings at 'Tennessee' throughout the summer of 1968.

Notes

1 *The London Gazette*, 5 June 1936.
2 A. C. Dixon had four children: Clarence Howard, known as Howard, who died in childhood; Abner Faison, known as Faison; Mary and Clara. Clara married Frank Richardson who was viewed as a spiritual replacement son for Howard, as Clarence had baptized Frank soon after the death of his son Howard.
3 Passenger lists—ancestry.org
4 Dixon, Helen Cadbury Alexander, *A. C. Dixon: A Romance of Preaching*, (New

York and London: Putnam's Sons, 1931), an inscription at the beginning of the book.

5 *The Brooklyn Daily Eagle*, New York, Saturday February 11th, 1928.

6 Dixon, Helen, C. A., *University Baptist Church, Baltimore, MD., Historic Sketch 1917–1926*, 1927. By kind permission of Wisconsin Historical Society Library, Madison, Wisconsin.

7 Dixon, Helen, C. A., *Intercession for Revival*, (Chicago, Ill., USA: The Bible Institute Colportage Association (Moody Press), 1927).

8 Ibid., p. 4.

9 The Pocket Testament League, Australia History online.

10 Philip E. Howard Jr. reported in an article entitled, 'The Times Party at the British Keswick', of his meeting many notable Christians at the Keswick Convention, one of whom was Helen Cadbury Alexander Dixon. *The Sunday School Times*, September 26th, 1931.

11 Sit, Amy, The Rib, (Harrison, Arkansas: New Leaf Press, Inc., 1977), p. 122.

12 Samuel, Leith, *A Man Under Authority, LEITH SAMUEL, The autobiography*, (Reading, Berks, UK: Christian Focus Publications, 1993), p. 46.

13 Ibid., p. 47.

14 Stanley Jebb in his Archive for February 27, 2018, 'Alethinos Reflections', Just another WordPress.com weblog. https://stanleyjebb.wordpress.com/2018/02/

15 The Second World War.

16 January 10, 1940. Personal papers, with the kind permission of N. Bradley, Helen's great nephew.

17 From a telephone conversation with C. Mary Penny, Helen's great niece.

18 The hymns of which we know she wrote are, 'After the shadows have passed away', and 'Over the Jasper Sea', although its first line is, 'There's a city bright and fair'. Helen wrote verses 3 and 4 of Jessie Pounds' hymn, 'Anywhere with Jesus'. 'All unseen the Master walketh', was adapted by Helen. Helen added stanzas to 'Jesus is our Captain' and added some stanzas to Kurtz's hymn, 'Jesus the Saviour is calling today'. 'Tell of Christ who saves from sin', was written with Carrie Breck (sometimes known as

Mrs Frank Breck. Helen added one stanza to Robert Lowry's hymn, 'Where is my wandering boy tonight?'. She also added stanzas to William Witter's hymn, 'While Jesus whispers to you'. Annie Louisa Walker and Helen wrote 'Work for the night is coming'.

19 Verses 3 and 4 were added by Helen Alexander but not all editions of this hymn have both these verses.

20 Jessie Pounds' hymn 'Anywhere with Jesus' Helen wrote verses 3 and 4. 'All unseen the Master walketh' was adapted by Helen; 'Jesus is our Captain' Helen added stanzas; 'Jesus the Saviour is calling today' Helen added some stanzas to Kurtz's hymn; 'Tell of Christ who saves from sin', written with Carrie Breck or sometimes known as Mrs Frank Breck; 'Where is my wandering boy tonight?' Helen added two stanzas to Robert Lowry's hymn; 'While Jesus whispers to you" Helen added stanzas to William Witter's hymn; 'Work for the night is coming' Annie Louisa Walker and Helen wrote this. Not all editions have her extra stanzas in these hymns.

15 Helen's death

At the ripe old age of ninety-two, Helen Cadbury Alexander Dixon died peacefully on 1st March 1969 at her beloved 'Tennessee'—her English home since her marriage to Charles in 1904. She was buried in the same grave as her beloved first husband, Charles, at Lodge Hill Cemetery, Birmingham, along with their infant son. The inscription has the Bible reference of Romans 1:16: 'For I am not ashamed of the gospel of Christ: for it is the power of God unto salvation to everyone that believeth; to the Jew first, and also to the Greek.' This Bible text was her signature Bible reference, just as Charles had 2 Timothy 2:15; therefore, when she wrote a letter, she signed her name and then added the verse and the reference.[1] Members of the Cadbury family and a few close friends attended the simple service at the graveside. Lt Col Berry, from the Salvation Army, read 1 Cor. 15.

In a Salvation Army report of the funeral, the connection with the Salvation Army and Helen's support of their work and her good relationships, not only with the local army members but also its important leaders, is evident:

Helen's signature

Helen's gravestone

Mrs Dixon was the eldest daughter of the late Mr Richard Cadbury, one of the two noted Cadbury brothers. She was keenly interested in The Salvation Army and generously supported its work. The Founder and General and Mrs Bramwell Booth received hospitality in her home. Lieut. Colonel Berry was also one of three speakers at the memorial service held in the Friends' Meeting House, Stirchley.

By Sidney Williams, Editor-in-Chief, I.H.Q.[2]

The simple service by the graveside included two hymns: firstly, 'The Lord's my shepherd', sung to the tune Crimond, and afterwards, 'Peace! Perfect peace!'

Memorial service

Later, a memorial service was held at the Friends' Meeting House, Stirchley, which was filled with many friends who came to remember 'the large-hearted woman who had drawn each one into her own circle'.[3] Informally, various guests participated in the service to pay tribute, to pray or praise. Rev. Peter Morgan, who had written a thesis on Moody and Sankey and Torrey and Alexander, and who had previously discussed Alexander's work with Helen; Edward J. Smith, the International Director of the Pocket Testament League; and Lt Col Berry all spoke at the service. Mr Smith spoke of her 'spiritual fruitfulness' and that her life seemed to have a 'chain reaction', giving the example of the PTL work. Ivy M. Lawrence, friend and PTL worker, said that Helen had a 'heart of gold' but was also a formidable lady who was a perfectionist and expected high standards of others. But 'she was generous to a fault and had a gift of humour.... and will be sorely missed.'[4] At the Friends Meeting House, Stirchley, a further two hymns were sung: 'No Burdens Yonder' and 'The Glory Song'. The first hymn was written by Ada R. Habershon, a close friend who had written most of her hymns for Charles Alexander's missions from 1905 until her death in 1918. Ada had even discussed with Helen about the need for a hymn to reflect not just the resurrection and the future glory but the present glory and experiencing it now; consequently, she wrote an extra verse for the 'Glory Song':

> When by the gift of His infinite grace,
> I midst redeemed ones by faith take my place,
> Even down here, as I look on His face,
> This very moment is glory for me.[5]

But Habershon's hymn, which was chosen for Helen's memorial service, emphasized, like the 'Glory Song', that in heaven there would be no more sorrow or burdens. These two hymns were significant not only because of the words but the associations. Firstly, there was the friendship and hymn writing of Ada Habershon for the Alexanders and secondly, the great identification which the 'Glory Song' by Charles H. Gabriel had with Charles Alexander and his missions.

Also in the memorial service, a sonnet which Helen had written for her mother, Emma, in the year after the death of her father Richard, in 1889, was read:

> Dear God,
> Who sendest us both joy and pain,
> Teach us in both to recognise Thy hand;
> For over all Life's change of smiles and tears
> Hangs a thick veil of mystery; and when
> Our inner sight is blinded, and we grope
> For reasons in the twilight of our souls,
> By which to solve the puzzle Life presents
> All seems capricious, Till at length, the sun
> Of Thy great Love in rising on our hearts
> Pierces the veil; and in the chequered shade
> We slowly learn to understand Thy plan
> Of intermingled grief and happiness.
> The cup of sorrow still is hard to drink;
> But Thou dost share it, and our trembling hearts
> Grow stronger to endure the agony.
> How gladly, if the cup be full of joy
> We take, as from a Father's loving hand
> And find refreshment in the pure sweet draught.[6]

Two texts accompanied the memorial order of service:

'I have fought the good fight. I have finished the course. I have kept the faith' (2 Timothy 4:7), and 'Well done, good and faithful servant; enter thou into the joy of thy Lord' (Matthew 25:23).

Helen's legacies

Helen left her earthly home of 'Tennessee', Birmingham, for a more glorious, heavenly home. She had shared the gospel of salvation with many people and, through the work of the Pocket Testament League which she started as a young girl, shared the gospel through the Scriptures across the world. Helen left 'Tennessee', her earthly home, for a better one but, even in death, she wanted to leave her 'Tennessee' for the benefit of others, just as she had done in life. She left wishes in her will for it to be used as a home for the elderly. Unfortunately, it was found to be unsuitable, so it was demolished and a new 'Tennessee' was built in its place, forming sheltered accommodation for 73 people, including 32 flats plus a staff house and a staff flat. The Birmingham Council for Old People agreed to take over the responsibility for its running and in its place is a nursing home.

Although Helen's estate was left financially healthy, by the time all the estate duties and taxes were paid, along with the generous annuities, legacies, gifts and expenses, there was not as much money as first thought. Yet, the trustees managed to distribute gifts and to provide the long-term annuities to all the named people and causes and then, to give any excess to smaller causes. For instance, £5000 was given to Leighton Park School, Reading, for new buildings

'New' Tennessee sheltered housing booklet

including a music department and its resources, and also monies were left for the Selly Oak Colleges. The larger monies were distributed to the Pocket Testament League and The Friends Service Council: this was subdivided to support specific works at an international centre in Madagascar; costs towards modernization of the Friends International Centre, London; Brummana High School, Lebanon; a new Quaker House in Geneva; and of course, the three large expenditures of the Helen Dixon House, the new 'Tennessee' and the Salvation Army Community Centre.

Helen had created a legacy in the form of 'The Helen Dixon Charitable Trust', which was created for the purpose of supporting appropriate charitable works and subsequently, a home for homeless people was named the Helen Dixon House in Birmingham. The house provided flatlets for 28 women and later, after its opening, Helen's sisters, Daisy and Beatrice, who flew in from Holland, came to visit this home. This house was under the auspices of the YWCA and was built at the cost of £100,000. The building was in Alcester Road, not too far from the original 'Tennessee'.

Helen's lengthy will shows her thoughtfulness for others and the large extent of her kindness to family members, employees and friends, with a large number of named individuals benefitting from her assets. Her stepchildren and her step-grandchildren were provided for, as well as closer family members. Her will did not forget some nieces of Charles, and the children of her late uncle, Samuel Wilson, who resided in New Zealand. It also provided sums of money and long-term annuities for individual employees. A property which Helen owned in Yarningdale Road, Birmingham, was to be given to her employees, Mr and Mrs Leonard Smith. She had even thought about any cars which she might own and, if they were still in her possession, they were to be inherited by her chauffeur. Her will is reflective of her thoughtfulness—an example being £100 left to 'Miss Enid Prichard ... in recognition of her kind help with the household wages'.[7]

In 1974, the opening of the Salvation Army Community Centre was recorded in the local Birmingham newspaper, and it acknowledged the receipt of funds from the Helen Cadbury Dixon Trust.

The following is an excerpt from the opening of the Salvation Army Community Centre:

> The three-storey Birmingham Citadel Community Centre, and divisional headquarters, in St Chads, Queensway was opened by the British Commissioner of the Salvation Army, Cmdr. Geoffrey Dalziel...
>
> The £220,000 building incorporates a flat and several offices.
>
> Another part of the building is the youth room, where it is hoped a community service can be provided for the children of nearby Newtown.
>
> Money for the building was raised by donations and local members contributed £20,000, partly by holding jumble sales.
>
> The Helen Cadbury Alexander Dixon Trust made the largest contribution—£80,000,—and Birmingham City Council contributed towards the community centre within the citadel. But another £3,000 is still needed towards the cost.[8]

'Helen's hymn'

Music had been central to Helen's life. From an early age she had enjoyed singing; she had learnt to play the piano and other instruments and these pleasures had continued to the end of her life. Music was a pivotal part of her married life with Charles and their work. The production of hymn books, particularly the Alexander hymnals, was a legacy of their lives. Helen wrote two verses which she added to Jessie Pounds'(Brown) hymn: 'Anywhere with Jesus'. These verses of hers (see below), reflect her personal life, a life lived for her Saviour the Lord Jesus Christ. They also depict her motto, work and mission as shown in her signature Bible text of Romans 1:16: 'For I am not ashamed of the gospel of Christ, for it is the power of God unto salvation to every one that believeth.' Finally, they confirm her future hope and certainty of her heavenly home with Christ. This was the theme in 'The Glory Song', which was so closely associated with her and Charles.

> Anywhere with Jesus, over land or sea,
> Telling souls in darkness of salvation free;
> Ready as He summons me to go or stay,
> Anywhere with Jesus when He points the way.
>
> *Anywhere, anywhere! Fear I cannot know;*
> *Anywhere with Jesus I can safely go.*
>
> Anywhere with Jesus I can go to sleep,
> When the dark'ning shadows round about me creep,
> Knowing I shall waken nevermore to roam;
> Anywhere with Jesus will be home, sweet home.[9]

Helen certainly did go over land and sea many times to proclaim the gospel of the Lord Jesus Christ and she at last found her home, sweet home with her Saviour, the Lord Jesus Christ. Helen Cadbury Alexander Dixon was a soldier for Christ and certainly no chocolate soldier.

Notes

1 See the transcription of her letter to the Pocket Testament League, p. 189.
2 *The War Cry* No. 4404 (Official organ of the Salvation army in Canada and Bermuda).
3 *The Life of Faith*, March 13, 1969, p. 10–11.
4 *The Life of Faith*, March 13, 1969, p. 10–11.
5 Habershon, Ada R., *Ada R. Habershon: A Gatherer of Fresh Spoil*, (London: Morgan and Scott Ltd., 1918), p. 48.
6 By kind permission of the Cadbury family—C. Mary Penny, Helen's great niece.
7 Helen Cadbury Alexander Dixon's will.
8 *The Birmingham Post*, November 4th, 1974.
9 183 Timeless Truths hymns, number 262. ttps://library.timelesstruths.org/music/Anywhere_with_Jesus/

*Helen Cadbury Alexander
Dixon*

Appendix 1

'Christ is thy Light': a hymn written by Richard Cadbury, Helen's father.

Christ is thy Light, O wand'rer, tempest-tossed!
The beacon-light is pointing to thy rest;
Dark is the night, and rocky is the coast,
But sure it shines above the billow's crest;
Christ is thy Light!

Christ is thy Strength, O faint and weary soul!
Thy strife is vain; embrace without delay
The grace that pleads with thee to make thee whole;
Who by His blood has washed thy sins away;
Christ is thy Strength.

Christ is Thy Guide, O pilgrim seeking rest!
He gently bids thee open wide the door
For Him to enter in and be thy guest;
O trust and follow Him forevermore;
Christ is thy Guide.

Christ is thy Hope! O cling to self no more,
No more to hopes which flatter and decay,
But to the Rock that stands the tempest's roar,
On which thy trembling ark will find a stay;
Christ is thy Hope!

Christ is thy King! He wore the crown for thee,
A crown of thorns, a diadem so meet;

O bow before His love that made thee free,
And humbly cast thy crown before His feet;
Christ is thy King!

Appendix 2

The institutions represented at Richard Cadbury's funeral

Among the many bodies and institutions who appointed deputations to attend Richard Cadbury's funeral, were the following:

- Severn Street, Class XIV. (George Cadbury's class).
- British and Foreign Bible Society.
- Moseley Hall Convalescent Home.
- Gospel Temperance Mission.
- Police Court Mission.
- United Kingdom Alliance.
- United Kingdom Alliance (Birmingham Auxiliary).
- Birmingham Band of Hope Union.
- Midland Temperance League.
- Sunday Closing Association (Midland District).
- Workhouse Drink Reform League.
- Worcester Diocesan Church of England Temperance Society.
- Birmingham Temperance Society.
- Temperance Social Union.
- National Vigilance Association.
- Birmingham Sunday School Union.
- Birmingham Council of the Evangelical Free Churches.
- West Midland Federation of Evangelical Free Churches.
- National Temperance League.
- Birmingham Peace Society.
- Moseley Road Wesleyan Cricket Club.
- Lozells Street Wesleyan Mission.
- The World-wide Circle of Prayer.

- Birmingham Young Men's Christian Association.
- Birmingham Medical Mission.
- Birmingham Town Mission.
- National Society for the Prevention of Cruelty to Children.
- Children's Hospital.
- National Liberal Federation.
- Birmingham Liberal Association.
- Allotments Association.
- North Worcestershire Liberal Association.
- King's Norton District Council.
- Birmingham School Board.
- Birmingham and Midland Education League.
- Birmingham Board of Guardians.
- Sir Josiah Mason's Orphanage.
- *Deritend Ward Relief Association.
- Messrs. T. Cook & Sons.
- The Salvation Army.
- The Bournville Mothers' Meeting.
- **The P. S. A.
- Sherbourne Road Board School.
- Bordesley Ward Liberal Association.

The original number of thirteen stewards was augmented by a couple of hundred assistant stewards from Bournville Works and Moseley Road Adult School, who lined the lane from the chapel to the grave.

*Deritend was a ward of Birmingham

** The Pleasant Sunday Afternoon group

Appendix 3

The nieces' scrapbook

This scrapbook was the one given to Joy Cadbury, used with permission by Mary Penny, Joy's daughter and Helen's great niece.

Page 1.
Log of the niece-party
Thursday, September 4th, 1919

The first arrival was Joy, from Wast Hills. With her came her Mother, also John and Alan, and Ken Wilson—in his military uniform. Soon afterwards Betty and Christine came from Stretton Croft. It was a wet afternoon, and we went down to the tea-sheds (where white rings were painted on the asphalt floor, as on the deck of a ship) and had a good game of deck-quoits. We let poor old Kelly, the brown-eyed, brown-haired setter, out of his kennel, and he was happy to be with a family party, after his lonely years. After a while Geraldine arrived with her Mother, from Southfield, and Uncle Charles went into town to meet Eveline and Beth at New Street station, and bring them to Tennessee. We had a merry tea-party in the drawing-room and began to get really acquainted with each other.

At supper-time, in the dining-room, Uncle Charles started us on a game of guessing ages, and much merriment was caused in guessing the age of Mr Thomas, who has been staying at Tennessee to recover from his long months in hospital, after serving in France. The one whose guess was nearest won a prize of chocolate.

After supper we gathered round the piano in the drawing-room.

Leonard Voke (Uncle Charles' twenty-year-old pianist) played to us, and then we all learned to sing 'We journey to a City', of which Leonard has composed the music.

We had great fun over a game called 'Tumble in', and everybody laughed as we watched one after another take the board and steer the wobbly little cylinders into the best numbered holes or see them drop unbidden into the workhouse or topple over unto the cleft at the end of the board. Later Mr Thomas gave us his wonderful recitation of 'How Bill Adams won the Battle of Waterloo', followed by 'Sneezing', which made us all feel as if we had a cold in the head. Then came a hymn and a word of prayer, and we all went upstairs to our various rooms for the night. Aunt Helen came to tuck us up and give us a final good-night kiss.

Friday, September 5th, 1919

It was quite exciting on Friday morning to wake and find ourselves all together. Soon we were gathered in the hall for prayer and had a merry time at breakfast. Before we got up from the table Uncle Charles asked Mr Thomas to go out and fetch a green book—'Poems you ought to know'. He soon brought it and Geraldine read aloud to us the beautiful poem by William Cullen Bryant called 'Thanatopsis'.

After breakfast, Aunt Helen and Mr Thomas were busy, so Uncle Charles showed us a number of interesting photographs. Later on, he read us some more poems. Amongst these by J. W. Riley was one called 'The Raggedy Man'. There was also a funny one called 'The Pessimist', by Ben King, and a dear little poem in the coloured people's dialect called 'Po' li'l lamb' by the negro poet, Paul Lawrence Dunbar.

Just before lunch time there was a buzzing sound outside, which proved to be Billy Butler's motorcycle. He had come to lunch with us. Uncle Charles kept us all busy at the luncheon table. He read us the following funny joke from Punch:

A medical officer, coming out of a military hospital, asked a V.A.D. how she succeeded in getting one of the patients to gargle. 'Oh,' she said, 'I just told him to take a mouthful, throw his head back, and make a noise in his throat like an officer.'

Uncle Charles made us recite a verse of poetry one after the other. After that everybody in turn had to tell one of the funniest stories they had ever heard. Christine said she did not know any funny story, but Mr Thomas promised that whatever story she told he would laugh at, even if nobody else did. When her turn came, she told a little story, and immediately Mr. Thomas set off into an irrepressible artificial laugh. 'Ha, Ha, Ha! Ho. Ho. Ho! He, He. He!' It seemed so real that soon everybody else was laughing too. Mr. Thomas went on until we were holding our side with merriment. Then all of a sudden, he stopped, and his face was as solemn as could be. Christine's look of astonishment made us laugh all the more. While we were having dessert, who should pass the window but Aunt Edith and Marjorie Frankland, Billy's fiancée. They had come over by train from Barnt Green, and we brought them into the dining room to have some fruit with us. Aunt Edith was made to tell a funny story which was as follows:

The whole Butler family had gone to Dunwich for a holiday. As there was plenty of heather there, they took with them one of the bee-hives from Stretton Croft, hoping to get some good heather honey. They set it up on the moor, and one day Mr Cephas Butler, and Uncle Arnold were bending over the hive examining it. All of a sudden the others saw Uncle Arnold stand upright and run like mad, for no apparent reason whatsoever. He jumped over the bosses of heather and tore along until at last he stopped and came back. When the others should to ask what was the matter, he called back, 'A bee was after me!'

Friday (contd.)

After lunch we all went into the drawing room and Mr. Voke played us the music of a song, 'Tennessee', composed by Mr Harkness in 1910. The words were written by Mr. Rock. After that we tried over a new short chorus, 'Saved and Kept', the words and music of which Leonard Voke had just written.

Uncle Charles had decreed that everybody was to compose at least one verse of original poetry, to be recited or read later in the day; so, we all scattered to various parts of the house for the next hour to get our brains to work.

About 4 o'clock others began to arrive. Mr Cephas Butler came from Stretton Croft, and soon afterwards Mother and Father came, bringing with them John, Alan, and Constance. We had an old-fashioned high tea in the dining room—a family party of nineteen. There was a small table in the alcove for John, Alan, Beth, Christine and Connie—John acting as chairman. Tea over we adjourned to the drawing room, where everyone had to read or recite the original poem composed during the afternoon. Leonard Voke's contribution was a chorus, 'Saved and Kept'. Aunt Edith had written some beautiful verses, and Beth and Christine had composed a most weird ghost poem! The four girls, Cherry, Joy, Eveline and

Betty, had made up a 'Song of the Nieces'. They stood in a row, each reciting her own verse in turn. Then we all went up to put on our cloaks, to make excursion down to the tea-sheds, where Mr Thomas was ready to give us an interesting show of lantern slides. The big old nursery table from Uffculme was pushed into a corner, with a garden seat upon it, this forming special gallery seats.

The pictures carried us back to many happy days, as there were a number of family scenes, some of them showing Auntie Bee and Uncle Kees, with little Helen and Emma, when they were living at 'Tennessee'. There were numbers of others, showing 'Tennessee' in summer and winter, and with various groups of people in them. A picture of Stretton Croft brought back memories of a happy day there, when seven of Uncle Charlie's 'Kentucky boys' had been invited. Amongst the most interesting slides were a series showing dear old Uffculme in the days when Grandmother was there, and she herself was seen in some of the pictures. It was half past nine before we left the tea-sheds and went up to the house for some hot cocoa, before the various guests departed. We sang 'Saved and Kept' together in a chorus, and then all went upstairs for the night's rest.

Saturday, September 6th, 1919

Glorious sunshine greeted our waking eyes on Saturday and made me all the more ready for a bright and happy day. Some of us were downstairs early and gathered around the piano in the drawing room, where Leonard Voke made us all laugh by playing 'The Last Rose of Summer' with the highest note a semitone flat, pretending that the piano was out of tune; then he made us feel like toothache by a most excruciating performance, playing in one key with one hand, and another key with the other, each quite correct in itself, but forming appalling discords together. Betty then gave him a lesson in 'Chopsticks' to change his thoughts. By this time all were down for prayers, and we gathered in the hall with the maids, to sing, and read, and pray together. When breakfast was over Aunt Helen was busy so Uncle Charles invited all the nieces into the library, where he said he was going to give us a lecture on 'How to choose a Husband'. It sounded funny to begin with, but after a while we found ourselves talking about things that took some good hard thinking—about our influence over our friends at school and elsewhere, and what the real purpose of our lives has been and is to be.

To our surprise the morning slipped away before we knew it, and we had only time for a hurried constitutional in the garden to get up an appetite for dinner. We were all glad to welcome Dorothy, who had been too busy at Bournville to join us before, till then. She was not allowed to escape the tests of the day before and had to do her share in telling a funny story. Later on, each one round the table had to say who amongst the people they knew, outside the family and relatives, had made a deep helpful impression on their lives. Joy told of her friend Nell Bain; Geraldine of Dr Rendel Harris; Eveline could not mention anyone in particular outside the family circle, but Betty spoke of Miss Milliner as one who helped her. Mr. Thomas mentioned George T. B. Davis, the International Secretary of the Pocket Testament League, as the one whose unfailing efforts, year after year, to win souls to Christ, had left an impression on his mind which could not be erased. Leonard Voke spoke of Dr. J. Wilbur Chapman, through whose preaching he had learned so much of Christ and the Word of God. Dorothy told of Mary Snowden

Braithwaite. Then Aunt Helen told us about Mrs. McAnlis, the Secretary of the Pocket Testament League in New York, whose husband died after they had been married only three years, and of her sunny sweetness of character, and brave devotion to her work for Christ; also of Miss Higgins, the famous 'sunshine invalid' of Melbourne, Australia. Dorothy gave us two more beautiful stories, one of them about two little boys at the Moseley Road Institute.

Saturday (contd.)

The wonderful sunshine was too tempting for us to stay long indoors, and we were soon busy on the lawn with a game of croquet. Meanwhile Mr. Thomas stalked us with his camera, as though we were valuable game, and got some pictures which will crystallize the happy day in our memories. About half-past four, tea was brought out into the garden, and we had a merry time over it, only disturbed by the visits of some greedy wasps, and the appearance of an enormous worm, which Chrissie thought was a snake.

After tea, Mr. Thomas had to arrange us in groups for some more photographs. Then we scattered again for a most energetic game of hide-and-seek, using the little verandah leading out of the hall as 'Home'. Beth and Chris were the seekers. Leonard Voke led them a great dance by hiding on the roof of the Log Hut. When he squatted down against the roof it was impossible to see him from below, and the two girls were much mystified by hearing him call every now and again, and yet not being able to trace him. As he had provided himself with a nice pocket-full of apples, he was quite happy, but, when at last he tried to descend to get 'home', they saw him and ran their prize to the earth.

Everyone put on their prettiest dresses for supper that evening, and we gave a hearty welcome to Uncle Arnold, who came to make up for having to be away the day before. He enjoyed Len's playing upon the piano, and after supper we had about half-an-hour of singing and music. Uncle Arnold tried to make all kinds of explanations about the story Aunt Edith had told about his running away from a bee, but only succeeded in making us laugh all the harder. For Uncle Arnold's benefit, and as an extra treat for us all, Mr. Thomas said he would show us some more pictures on the screen, so we all trooped down to the tea-sheds. This time we saw some wonderful pictures of New York, showing the great skyscraper buildings, and views of the city from the top of the Singer building, and from ships in the harbour. Some of the slides showed the elevated railways. Other pictures were shown of Switzerland, and of the Canadian Rockies, and of our lovely English Lake District. At the close came the greatest surprise of all, for suddenly Mr. Thomas put upon the screen pictures of ourselves playing croquet, which he had only taken that very afternoon!!!

It was hard to tear ourselves away to bring Uncle Arnold up to the house, and then it was time for us all to seek our cosy beds.

Sunday, September 7th, 1919

Dorothy was up betimes on Sunday morning, and before we had prayers, she had finished her breakfast and was off on her bicycle to take her class of women in Miss Cave's Early Morning School at the Moseley Road Friends' Institute.

At prayers, Uncle Charles asked us to recite a favourite verse from the Bible, which was very helpful to us all. This happy few minutes of singing and Bible-reading and prayer each morning as a united household, drew us together and helped us all through the day.

After breakfast we had to hurry to be ready for going down to the Friends' Meeting at Moseley Road. We seemed quite a little army as we marched into the Meeting, which was very helpful time of worship. The walk back gave us a good appetite for dinner, at which we all enjoyed presents from other homes. A lovely basket of mushrooms and tomatoes had been brought from Wast Hills the day before, and a delicious vegetable marrow had been sent from Stretton Croft. Another treat was some fresh sweet butter from Bilthoven, also a Dutch cheese, sliced thin, as is eaten in Holland.

After dinner Uncle Charles called us all into the drawing room and said he wanted us to do something for him before we went upstairs for a Sunday afternoon rest. He gave round some pencils and pieces of paper, and Leonard Voke brought in the afternoon-tea tables so that we each could have one to write on. Then Uncle Charles said, 'I want you to take a quarter of an hour to write down your own answer to the question, "What is a Christian?"' This set us all thinking, and for the next few minutes the room was very quiet except for the sound of our pencils. When all had finished, the sheets were handed to Uncle Charles. None were signed, and after mixing them up a little, he read the definitions aloud one after the other.

(There were some pages of definitions of 'What is a Christian?' by the nieces that are not included here.)

Sunday (contd.)
About half past three we all trooped upstairs. Cherry, Joy, Eveline,

Betty, Beth and Christine went with Aunt Helen into the Green Room. In spite of there being two comfortable beds and a sofa everybody chose to lie flat on the floor with rugs and cushions, while Aunt Helen read aloud to us. She first read us three stories from 'The Traveller's Guide'. The first was 'John 3:16', the story of a little street-Arab who found Christ through that wonderful verse. The next was a Californian story, called 'The man who died for me", while the third was 'The last three Pages of an Officer's Diary'. The diary had been written by a man who had been suddenly told, by a doctor, that he could not live for more than a month at the outside. It showed how the values of everything were changed to a man who had been living an ordinary, gay, careless life. After having the first doctor's opinion confirmed by others, this man of the world tells of his search for the only things that mattered in the light of Eternity, and how he was finally led to Christ, by a man who cleaned the shoes and did odd jobs in the hotel. The last entry, written sixteen days after the doctor's declaration, was: 'Thirteen days ago I wrote "I have found Him!" ... Dr Tintern, you have opened the door of heaven to me.' A short entry follows: 'read 53rd chapter of Isaiah, 3rd John, and 4th and 5th of Romans.'

After these three stories from 'The Traveller's Guide', Aunt Helen read us a charming American tale, called 'Their Christmas Golden Wedding', by Caroline Abbot Stanley. It was then time to get ready for tea, which we had out in the Log Hut. Dorothy came back from Moseley Road just in time for tea. We sat a good while over it, and then enjoyed a stroll in the evening sunshine.

We had supper about eight o'clock, and then had some singing in the drawing room, taking each one's favourite hymn in turn. Then

Cherry read aloud to us, with beautiful expression, a most tender poem, called 'The Hebrew Mother' from the book, *Ezekiel and other poems*, by B. M. It is the story of Abijah, the little son of Jeroboam. The child fell ill, and his mother hastened in disguise to consult the blind old prophet Ahijah, in Shiloh. The Prophet rebuked her for her feigning, and after stern words from God with regard to the wickedness of Jeroboam, he said to the sorrowing mother: 'Arise thou therefore, get thee to thine own house: and when thy feet enter into the city, the child shall die' (1 Kings, 14:12). The poem pictures the agonising struggle of the royal mother to gather up courage to cross the threshold of the city gates, and tells of an angel sent to comfort her, and remind her of the prophet's words, that God in His loving mercy was taking her little one gently Home, before His stern judgments fell upon the house of Jeroboam. All Israel was to mourn for the child, and 'he only of Jeroboam' should be laid in a peaceful grave, for the Lord God of Israel had found 'some good thing', in the boy's heart towards Himself. Thus, learning to trust God's love, the mother was helped to go through her ordeal.

Sunday (contd.)

Our hearts were deeply stirred as Cherry read to us, and as she finished, Aunt Helen, suggested how helpful a chorus would be expressing that lesson of trust. Almost immediately Uncle Charles had suggested the words:

> I'll trust when I cannot see, Lord,
> I'll trust where I cannot see,
> No matter how dark the way may be,
> I'll trust where I cannot see!

We all bent our heads in prayer, asking that Leonard Voke might be given the right music for the words, and in a few moments, he began softly playing the music to the chorus, which he found on another page. It will always have a special meaning for us who were together the night it was written.

Uncle Charles then brought in a number of Workers' Testaments. Giving one to each, he asked us to open at a page, where under various headings, was a list of 'Some things which every unsaved person should know.' Under each heading were references to illustrative passages of Scripture. He showed us how to turn to the passages and use them in making the Way of Life clear to anyone anxious to find Christ. Then we spent a few minutes on another page, showing how to meet objections to an immediate decision to Christ, such as: 'Waiting to get better'; 'Too many hypocrites'; 'Too much to give up'; and so on. Those who wished to do so were invited by Uncle Charles to keep the Workers' Testament and continue to study; several of us gladly accepted it.

It was hard work to leave each other and go upstairs that night, for the day had been so happy and helpful. Several times we made a start to go, when a fresh question would be asked, or another verse of a hymn called for, but finally we made our way to our various rooms for the night.

Monday, September 8th, 1919

The house was astir early, with a grand rush on the bathrooms. Dorothy had an early breakfast by herself, as she had to be off to Bournville. At prayers we sang 'God will take care of You,' and Uncle Charles read Numbers 6:14–26, and also the first Psalm. In a word or two he showed how this Psalm gave the key to real solid prosperity, which comes through leaving undone three things mentioned in the first verse, and through the doing of the one thing spoken of in the second verse. He showed that it was not merely the doing of this thing, but enjoying to do it, which counted.

As soon as breakfast was over, everybody flew upstairs to get their bags packed, and then we had a grand assembly in the library for general report on our days together. Aunt Helen had been asked to write out our log for us, so we all tried to remember the happenings each day, and as we called out this thing or that, Leonard Voke acted as secretary and took down rough notes to help Aunt Helen. Just as we were finishing, a motor passed the window, bringing Aunt Geraldine, who had come for Cherry. We took her into the drawing-room where we all had some cocoa. Then we gathered round the piano and sang to her the new choruses and 'We journey to a City'.

Soon the good-byes began, and by lunch-time only Eveline and Beth were left. Uncle Charles took them to New Street in the afternoon and put them into their train for Worcester. The niece-party, to which we had all looked forward, was over, but it had brought much into our lives. We had grown to know each other, after the long separations of the war-time years. Best of all, we had helped each other into closer touch with the Lord Jesus Christ, and the memory of our happy days will not soon fade.

[My added note: The scrapbook was interspersed with various photographs of Tennessee, its weekend visitors and various activities as well as copies of hymns which had been sung.]

'Song of the Nieces'

Here from Barnt Green, Worcester, Brum,
All the joyful nieces come.
Uncle Charles has made us write
Poems with our main and might.
In the nursery we did sit,
Racking brains with foreheads knit,
Casting eyes around in vain,
While some fruit did us sustain.
This is all we can produce
As our brains are somewhat loose
After recitative dinner
Halfpennies flying for the winner.
Now our Aunt and Uncle here
We welcome back with thundering cheer,
We couldn't end this feeble lay
Without all yelling Hip Hurray.

Appendix 4

Alexander's hymnals:

The following is a list of some of Alexander's hymn books that he compiled or edited:

[There are various publications of these hymn books, which are slightly different according to their dates and places of publication, especially the British and the American versions of the hymn books. Of course, there were numerous song sheets published for the campaigns.]

- Alexander's Gospel Hymn Book 1–3
- Alexander's Gospel Solos
- Alexander's Gospel Songs 1–8
- Alexander's Gospel Songs and Solos
- Alexander's Hymns 1–4
- Alexander's Male Choir
- Alexander's New Revival Hymns 1–2
- Alexander's Revival Hymns 1–3
- Alexander's Revival Songs
- Alexander's Songs of the Gospel 1–3
- Conference Hymnal
- Foundation Hymns
- Gospel Songs of Distinction
- Hymnal of the Baltimore Conference on Christian Fundamentals
- Immanuel's Praise
- Montreat Hymns

- National Baptist Convention Hymnal
- Northfield Hymnals:
  - » No. 1, Ed. George Stebbins with Alexander's Supplement
  - » No. 2, Moody/Alexander
  - » No. 3, Moody/Alexander
- Revival Hymns
- Songs for the Service of Christ
- Songs of the Assembly, No. 1
- Victorious Life Hymns
- Work and Worship

Bibliography

Alexander, Helen Cadbury and Maclean, J. Kennedy, *Charles M. Alexander: A Romance of Song and Soul-winning,* (London: Marshall, 1920).

Alexander, Helen Cadbury, *Richard Cadbury of Birmingham,* (London: Hodder and Stoughton, 1906).

Bartlett, Percy W, *Barrow Cadbury, A Memoir,* (London: Bannisdale Press, 1960).

Boeke, Beatrice C., *Emma Richard Cadbury 1846–1907,* (place of publication not identified, 195?).

Cadbury, Deborah, *Chocolate Wars: from Cadbury's to Kraft—200 years of sweet success and rivalry*, (London: Harper Collins, 2010 imprint).

Cadbury, Richard ('Historicus', pseudo), *Cocoa: all about it*, (Birmingham: Samson, Low and Marston, 1892).

Cadbury, William A. and Henry J., *The Cadbury Pedigree*, (Birmingham, 1904), this includes Richard Cadbury's genealogical charts which he researched and are handwritten by him—they form part of 'The Family Book'.

Chinn, Carl, *The Cadbury Story,* (Studley, Warwickshire: Brewin Books Ltd., 1998).

Cole, Keith, *Fred P. Morris and other Bendigo Hymnwriters*, (Bendigo: Keith Cole Publications, 1989).

Cole, Keith, *Robert Harkness, The Bendigo Hymnwriter,* (Bendigo: Keith Cole Publications, 1988).

Crosfield, John F., *A History of the Cadbury Family (2 volumes)*, (London: J. F. Crosfield, 1985).

Crosfield, A. J. & G., *A man in shining armour: the story of the life of William Wilson, M.R.C.S. and L.R.C.P., missionary in Madagascar, secretary of the Friends' Foreign Mission Association,* (London: Headley Brothers, Undated, possibly 1911).

Davis, George T. B., *Torrey and Alexander: The study of World-wide revival,* (New York: Fleming Revell, 1905).

Davis, George, T. B., *The Pocket Testament League Around the World,* (Philadelphia: The Pocket Testament League, 1910).

Davis, George T. B., *Twice around the World with Alexander, Prince of Gospel Singers*, (New York: Christian Herald, 1907).

Dixon, Helen, C. A., *Intercession for Revival,* (Chicago, Ill., USA: The Bible Institute Colportage Association (Moody Press), 1927).

Dixon, Helen, C. A., *University Baptist Church, Baltimore, MD., Historic Sketch 1917–1926.* (By kind permission of Wisconsin Historical Society Library, Madison, Wisconsin, 1927).

Dixon, Helen Cadbury Alexander, *A. C. Dixon: A Romance of Preaching,* (New York and London: Putnam's Sons, 1931).

Fox, Simon, *Helen Cadbury and Charles M. Alexander*, (London: Marshall Morgan and Scott Publications, 1989).

Gardiner, A. C., *Life of George Cadbury*, (London: Cassell and Company Limited, 1923).

Habershon, Ada R., *Ada R. Habershon: A Gatherer of Fresh Spoil,* (London: Morgan and Scott Ltd., 1918).

Hadley, Samuel H., *Down in Water Street*, (Conjurske Publications, 1907).

Hall, H. J., *Biography of Gospel Song and Hymns Writers*, (New York: Fleming H. Revell, 1914).

Gabriel, Charles Hutchinson, *Sixty Years of Gospel Song*, (Chicago, Illinois: Hope Publishing, not dated).

James, Leslie, *The Quaker Girl and her League,* (Exeter: Paternoster Press (for Pocket Testament League), 1986).

Joseph, Fiona, *Beatrice, The Cadbury Heiress Who Gave Away Her Fortune,* (Birmingham: Foxwell Press, 2012).

Maclean, John Kennedy, *Torrey and Alexander: the story of their lives,* (London: S. W. Partridge, 1905).

Maclean, John Kennedy, '*When Home Is Heaven': A Brief Sketch of the Home-Life of Mr & Mrs Charles M. Alexander,* (London: Marshall Brothers Ltd., 1922).

Murray, Iain H. *The Forgotten Spurgeon,* (Edinburgh, The Banner of Truth Trust, 1966, 1973).

Ottman, Ford C., *J. Wilbur Chapman, A biography,* (Garden City, New York: Doubleday, 1920).

Roberts, Philip L., '*Charlie' Alexander, A Study in Personality,* (London and Edinburgh: Fleming H Revell Company, 1920).

Samuel Leith, *A Man under Authority, Leith Samuel, The autobiography*, (Reading, Berks, UK: Christian Focus Publications, 1993).

Shinsato, Douglas T. and Urabe, Tadanori, *For that One Day: The memoirs of Mitsuo Fuchida, the Commander of the attack on Pearl*

Harbour, (Riverside, CT: Experience, Inc., 2011), a translation of his memoirs into English.

Sit, Amy, *The Rib*, (Harrison, Arkansas: New Leaf Press Inc., 1977).

Virgo, John J., *Fifty Years Fishing for Men*, (London: The Pilgrim Press, 1939).

Wilhoit, Mel R., *Alexander the Great: Or Just Plain 'Charlie'*, (The Hymn Volume 46, April 1995).

Wordsworth, Diane, *The life of Richard Cadbury: Socialist, Philanthropist and Chocolatier,* (Yorkshire—Philadelphia: Pen and Sword History, 2020).

Wordsworth, Diane, *A History of Cadbury,* (Yorkshire—Philadelphia: Pen and Sword History, 2018).

The Annual Monitor for 1908 GB and Ireland (U.S., UK and Ireland Quaker published memorials 1818–1919 (ancestrylibraryedition.co.uk; Ancestry.com))

Personal papers and artefacts:

By kind permission of the members of the Cadbury family—namely:

C. Mary Penny, great niece of Helen Cadbury Alexander Dixon.

N. Bradley, great nephew of Helen Cadbury Alexander Dixon.

Newspapers and magazines:

The Birmingham Post, November 4th, 1974.

The Brooklyn Daily Eagle, New York, Saturday 11 February 1928.

The Christian Herald and *Signs of Our Times*, 7 February 1924.

The Life of Faith, 13 March 1969.

The London Gazette, 5 June 1936.

The War Cry No. 4404, (Official organ of the Salvation army in Canada and Bermuda).

Internet sources:

Ancestry.co.uk

Archive.org

Find a grave. https://www.findagrave.com/

Hymnary.org

Stanley Jebb in his Archive for February 27, 2018, 'Alethinos Reflections', Just another WordPress.com weblog

Other materials:

Census

Copyright catalogues

Marriage certificates

Passenger lists

Helen Cadbury Alexander Dixon's will

List of photos

Front cover picture of Helen, 1904

Chapter 2 Helen's mother: Emma Jane Wilson
- Richard and Emma Cadbury around the time of their wedding
- Richard and Emma Cadbury (circa 1880)

Chapter 3 Helen and her siblings arrive
- Helen Cadbury as a child
- Helen, Emma and Daisy
- Plaque in Uffculme
- Present day Uffculme, previously Richard Cadbury's family home
- Barrow, Richard, Edith, William, Daisy, Richard—Back Row Helen, Jessie, Beatrice, Emma—Front Row (Left to right)

Chapter 4 A changed life
- Helen with Jessie, Edith, Daisy and Beatrice
- Helen around 1896

Chapter 5 The death of Helen's father
- Richard, Helen, Daisy and Beatrice in the Holy Land
- Richard Cadbury (1835–1889)

Chapter 6 Charles McCallon Alexander: His life before Helen
- Charles Alexander

Chapter 7 The romance of Helen and Charles

- Helen, Emma, Beatrice and Daisy (1904)

Chapter 8 The wedding and honeymoon of Helen and Charles

- The wedding of Helen and Charles

Chapter 9 Helen's health concerns

- 'Tennessee'
- Daisy, Emma and baby in 1907, Pakhoi
- Emma Cadbury's gravestone with Richard

Chapter 10 Trials of life

- The gravestone of Helen's baby

Chapter 11 Helen: Life back home at 'Tennessee'

- Photo of Helen's nieces with names
- Photo of Helen and her nieces
- 'Tennessee' the music sheet
- The fireplace at 'Tennessee'

Chapter 12 Charles' death

- The gravestone of Charles Alexander

Chapter 13 Marriage a second time around

- The wedding of Helen Cadbury Alexander and Clarence (A. C.) Dixon, by kind permission of the Evangelical Library, *The Christian Herald* and *Signs of Our Times*, 7 February 1924

Chapter 14 Helen's later life

- Helen (left) with her two sisters, Daisy (middle) and Beatrice
- Bournville Almshouses' Christmas party, 1948
- Robert Harkness's gravestone
- Helen and Daisy at Helen's 90th birthday
- Helen's 90th birthday celebrations
- Names of the guests in the photo of Helen's 90th

Chapter 15 Helen's death

- The signature of Helen Cadbury
- Helen's and Charles' gravestone
- Helen's gravestone inscription
- New 'Tennessee' sheltered housing leaflet
- Helen Cadbury Alexander Dixon